Manage to Lead

Seven Truths to Help You Change the World

Peter F. DiGiammarino

Manage to Lead

Seven Truths to Help You Change the World

Peter F. DiGiammarino

intelliVen

Intelligent Strategies. Successful Ventures.

Illustrations and icons by Maria Moon and Laura Dye

ISBN-13: 978-0-9891964-1-3

First Printing April 2013

Publisher: IntelliVen
               Suite 800
               1600 Tysons Blvd
               McLean, VA 22102

Subscribe at www.intelliven.com
Follow @intelliven

Cover design by Mari Foret / Foret Designs

Acknowledgements

The Manage to Lead Workbook exists only as a result of the help and support of many people. In particular I want to thank:

Peg DiGiammarino for unending support, drive, encouragement, and for patience to upgrade graphics and polish the material to the level its audience deserves.

Michael Broddle for first referring to my content as "disarmingly simple" and for encouragement and help to launch IntelliVen in the late '90s.

Alyssa Alfonso for inspiring the approach to what has become www.intelliven.com where virtually all of the content here-in was first posted.

Susan Dawson for helping to synthesize 38-hours of classroom material into the seven truths, sequencing them, linking them to Organization Development theory, and for making the material more useful and relevant to OD students.

Jaedra DiGiammarino for original photography in the one-line solutions to the nine-dot problem.

Fred Nader for inspiring the Leader Support Strategy, introducing me to the American University MS OD program, and for helping me to learn and apply so much of what he knows about organization development.

Katherine Farquhar and American University MSOD Cohorts 60, 62, 63, and 64 for allowing me to organize this material in front of them, providing feedback, applying what they learned, and sharing results.

Dan Ilisevich for help with financial material.

Chuck Work for patiently describing to me the leadership model espoused and exemplified by Elliot Richardson and that is reflected here-in as the Core Leadership Group.

Breanna DiGiammarino for the original idea to compile class notes and blogs into a workbook.

Ron Fell, Dr. Dory Hollander, and Karen Wall for helping me to become OD capable.

Mary Beth Robles for permission to use diagrams from her class project in Figures 18 and 19.

Ivan Selin, Charles Rossotti, Pat Gross, Reid Jackson, Brock Lending, Robert Acosta, Chris McGoff, Steve Lynott, Paul Brubaker, David Fout, Ed Bersoff, Mike Daniels, Tom Dixon, and Matt Flannery for helping me to develop this material and for giving me the opportunity to practice putting it to productive use.

Dean Clarkson and Meredith Feltus of University of Massachusetts Commonwealth Honors College for creating the opportunity for me to develop a one-hour summary presentation of this material.

Massachusetts Institute of Technology Sloan School of Management for introducing me to OD.

About the Author

Peter DiGiammarino develops and drives teams of high-potential, growth-driven professionals to build highly successful and fast-growing ventures based on offerings that solve specific important, pervasive, and persistent problems for tight markets.

Peter F. DiGiammarino

In addition to running companies, he has served public, private, private-equity-owned, and venture-capital-backed technology and service firms as an advisor and/or director and has consistently helped them to achieve sustained growth and performance. He is particularly skilled at helping top teams develop and align their corporate strategy with their operations. Peter also helps top teams implement governance, performance metric, incentive, and communications programs to ensure acceptance by their organization and success in the marketplace.

Peter has led successful ventures for The Carlyle Group, Novak Biddle, Paladin Capital Group, and Warwick Capital. Most recently he led Compusearch, a software provider to the US Federal Government, to a sale for nearly four times invested capital in five years.

He serves on the advisory board to the University of Massachusetts Commonwealth Honors College which he helped found. He is also Adjunct Professor of Organization Analysis, Strategy, and Development for the Master of Science in Organization Development (MSOD) program at American University in DC and was the 2012 University of Massachusetts Bateman Scholar in residence.

Peter earned a Bachelor of Science in Computer Science, Economics, and Mathematics from the University of Massachusetts at Amherst and an MBA from the Sloan School of Management with concentrated studies in Information Technology, Strategy, and Organization Development at the Massachusetts Institute of Technology.

Preface

Whether one wants to change **personal habits**, implement a new information system, improve a business process, get team members to work together, increase a community's appreciation for diversity, or even to topple a monarchy, taking actions driven by seven disarmingly simple truths will individually and collectively help achieve the goal.

Manage to Lead presents a framework to describe and assess *any* organization. It also provides a structured approach to plan and implement next steps for an organization as it strives for long-term growth and performance. Readers are invited to select a familiar organization on which to apply the tools and templates introduced throughout this workbook. Exercises in each chapter produce essential elements for the organization's annual strategic plan and lay the groundwork for implementing that plan.

In the role of chief executive, director, and manager, Peter DiGiammarino has led dozens of successful organizations, which ranged in maturity from initial concept stage to employing thousands of people and, collectively, generated billions of dollars in economic value and social impact. Educators at the Commonwealth College at the University of Massachusetts, Amherst and at the American University MSOD program in Washington, DC asked him to organize what he has learned into a form that can be shared with students.

The result is *Manage to Lead,* a workbook that brings to life his approach to guiding organizations to develop their operations to synchronize with their strategy. *Operations* refers to how to *PLAY* the game. *Strategy* refers to how to *WIN* the game. In *Manage to Lead*, Peter shows how to **turn strategy *into* operations** and to simultaneously **evolve strategy *from* operations** using seven truths gleaned from more than 30 years creating and growing organizations. His insights have been honed while teaching at a number of universities, most recently at American University in Washington, D.C., where he serves as an adjunct professor teaching Masters Students about leadership and organization analysis and strategy.

personal habits: Such as to: get fit, eat right, or stop smoking.

SEVEN ACTIONS

Get Clear

Get Aligned

Plan Change

Do & Review

Get Help

Grow

Focus

Table of Contents

Figures

Get Loose

Turn off autopilot and break through conventional boundaries to find new solutions to everyday problems.

Introduction

Why is it hard for some people to connect nine dots arranged in three rows of three with four straight lines and without retracing or lifting their writing implement?

Because it requires a change in the way they usually think.

If you find it hard or believe it is impossible, you are not alone. The reason it is hard is because in order to solve the puzzle a person has to think and operate in ways that are different than normal; or *outside the box*, as they say.

Before reading further, follow the instructions to solve the puzzle; first solve it with four lines, and then use just three lines. Finally, try to determine how many ways the puzzle can be solved with only one line. Compare your answers with those you study or work with and explore together how the exercise relates to individual and organization performance and growth. For example, Imagine an organization that connects dots and lines are its cost. How would such an organization maximize dot-connectedness while minimizing lines to make the most profit?

The nine-dot exercise dramatizes the effort it takes to break out of conventional ways of thinking and behaving to do things in new and different ways. Most of the time, people operate in *"autopilot mode"*; seeing and doing the same things in the same way over and over and time after time: get up in the morning, commute to and from the office, work, prepare and eat meals, watch television, surf the Web, interact with social media, and so on and so on.

While most of the time it may be just fine to live and work in autopilot mode, sometimes things go wrong. A good friend, for example, once **missed the beginning of an important meeting because he followed his car's GPS instructions and ended up at his home in Washington, DC instead of at a restaurant in Reston, VA because he never once looked to see where he was actually going along the way!**

It is important for a person, to step back every once in a while to look at things in a fresh light, see what is really there, and discover opportunities to improve. A leader needs to take a step back, along with his/her top team, to **get loose from the bonds of business** as usual to study and assess what is going on and to decide what must change. In some cases, and eventually perhaps in most cases, doing so becomes a matter of survival.

get loose from the bonds of business: Get Loose also launches Lewin's three stage change model: unfreeze—change—refreeze.

With the relentless press of day-to-day activity it is not easy to get loose. Here are some of the ways leaders make an effort to Get Loose:

- **Get off the job site and get clear of day-to-day pressures.**

- **Study how others, especially the best,** do the same work.

- Organizations work. Ask them what questions and ideas they have about how things work.

- Assign leaders to **study and reflect on parts of the organization other than those with which they are most familiar.**

- Ask leaders to brainstorm and **be open to new ideas.** Put the **planning horizon far enough out into the future that the constraints of the present melt away.**

- **Convene a forum of the best and brightest** from inside and outside the organization. Have each member of the forum review briefing materials about the organization today. Ask those present to **discuss the possibilities with no rules to constrain thinking.**

The *Manage to Lead* workbook introduces a structured approach to understand an organization, how it works and how it is doing. It lays out an approach to driving change in order to improve an organization.

Great leaders set a good example by being aggressively interested in new ideas that come from inside and outside the organization and encourage team members to do the same.

That is, they:

- Break through barriers,

- Adopt a fresh perspective,

- Challenge established norms, and possibly even

- Change the problem.

to Get Loose in order to: Manage to Lead using Seven Truths to Help You Change the World.

FOUR-LINE SOLUTION BREAKS THROUGH WALLS.

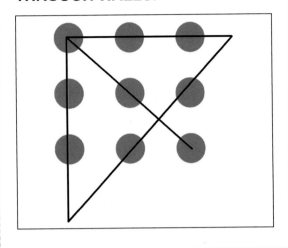

THREE-LINE SOLUTIONS REQUIRE A CHANGE IN PERSPECTIVE.

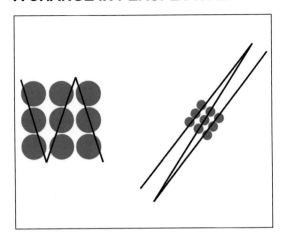

ONE-LINE SOLUTIONS PUSH NORMS EVEN FURTHER.

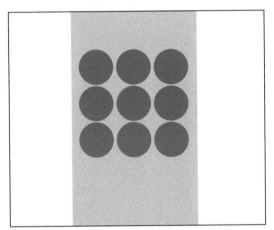

You can change the line to connect the dots with one line.

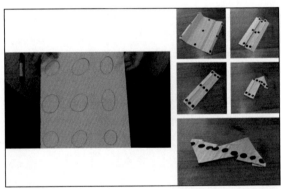

You can change the surface to connect the dots with one line.

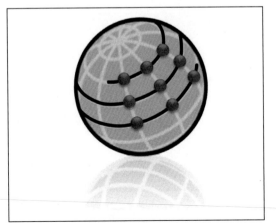

You can change perspective. In non-Euclidian geometry all lines are the same line and connect at infinity!

POINTS OF CONNECTION WITH NO-LINES

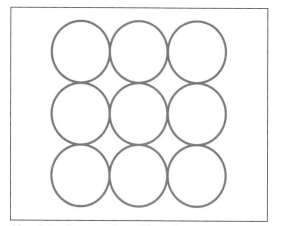

12 points of connection with no lines

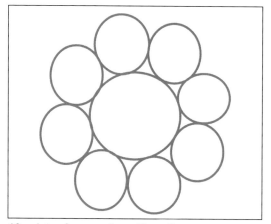

16 points of connection with no lines

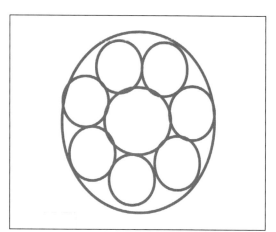

21 points of connection with no lines

Background

For decades organizations have sought and achieved productivity and performance improvement through information technology and process engineering initiatives. While these efforts streamlined and automated what organizations do to provide services and products, they often failed to also address many organization and people needs along the way. As a result, there is still a long way to go to achieve peak performance as suggested by the notional graphs presented in *Figures 1 and 2*.

While the next wave of performance improvement may come from mobile devices, network computing, big data, or any number of other things, it can also come, as suggested in *Figure 3*, principally from enhancing the way people perform as individuals and together in groups, teams, and organizational units. Leaders at all levels are learning to get the most from their organizations by developing each person and their teams to fulfill their potential to perform and grow.[1]

Unfortunately, the skills to effectively lead this next wave are not yet widely known or effectively taught and are difficult to figure out on-the-job even among bright and highly motivated professionals. They can, however, be learned. *Manage to Lead* content is rooted in the discipline of Behavioral Science as applied to real-world experiences by pioneering executives and cutting-edge executive coaches in public, private, venture-backed, and private-equity-owned for-profit and not-for-profit organizations. These executives and coaches have turned theory into highly effective practice and success with leaders in social, public, and commercial sector organizations of all sizes and stages of evolution.

Approach

Seven truths are presented in separate units with real examples and problems for readers to work on individually and in small groups. The material provides managers and those with business and Organization Development (OD) training with an opportunity to synthesize tools, techniques, and principles with organization operations and then

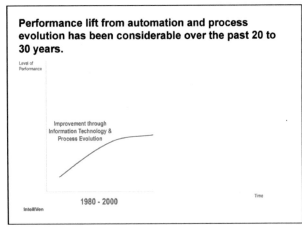

Figure 1. *Era of increasing productivity through automation and process evolution.*

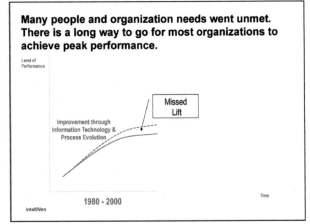

Figure 2. *Missed lift in performance.*

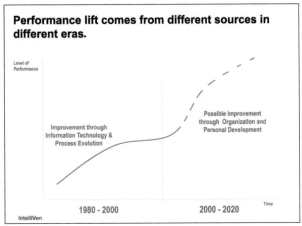

Figure 3. *Lift in performance in the future can come from organization and personal development.*

---

1 Patrick Lencioni makes a similar point in Advantage; see: http://www.tablegroup.com/oh/.

challenges them to apply what they have learned in order to improve real-world scenarios.

Financial and operating basics for organizations that aim to grow in scale and impact are introduced and readers are taught to think, plan, manage, and evolve strategically. Further, *Manage to Lead* explores how, once it is clear what one seeks to accomplish, proven tools, techniques, and principles can be used to purposefully help an organization progress from where it is to where it next desires to be in the longer-term quest to achieve a vision.

Readers select and examine a real organization to understand its strategy, how it works, and how well it is performing and then to develop strategic initiatives and a plan of Organization Development to progress towards a target state of their choosing.

Objectives

Manage to Lead Emphasizes:

- How important it is for leaders to be clear about what they seek to accomplish and why they want to accomplish it.

- How strategic thinking and strategic management can help leaders progress towards reaching goals.

- How implementing strategic initiatives requires clear goals; committed management time, attention, and resources; active and continuous stakeholder engagement; and limiting change to that which makes good sense in order to produce desired results.

- What it takes to effect and sustain planned change.

After reading *Manage to Lead* and completing its exercises, **leaders**, **consultants**, and **students** will have developed their ability to:

- Get and stay clear about what is most important to do next, build a coalition of support aligned with that intent, and form, launch, drive, communicate, track, and govern initiatives to accomplish targeted results.

- Describe and analyze an organization to determine what is most important to change next so as to increase the odds of better results, sooner, and to assess and advance its readiness for the change that comes with implementing strategic initiatives.

- Apply conceptual frameworks to facilitate strategic planning and guide organizations to achieve a desired result by promoting awareness, understanding, commitment, and action consistent with the required change.

- Build personal readiness to find and develop leaders who want to accomplish something specific and who benefit from applying OD tools, techniques, and principles to systematically help their organizations think and act strategically and to implement strategic initiatives.

leaders: Including: executives, and managers who are responsible for all or any part of an organization's performance.

consultants: Including strategy, management, and organization development consultants.

students: Especially MBA and MSOD students.

Manage to Lead provides insights for current and aspiring leaders who want to build "pizza-making businesses rather than make pizza.²" The topics covered here are not from your parents' textbook or an MBA lecture. What distinguishes this material is that it offers a chance to learn from those who have grown wiser from being in the trenches and who see both mistakes and success as opportunities to learn and grow.

Manage to Lead collects and codifies the work of many who have managed to lead in a variety of different businesses and situations. They paid attention to what did and did not work and why. They consolidated lessons learned and tuned key insights. Along the way they discovered some insightful truths about organizations and leaders that, once understood, can help people develop into effective leaders.

Manage to Lead's seven truths and the actions they drive can change the odds for success in simple yet powerful ways. Current and aspiring leaders are invited to **read, contemplate, discuss, develop their own points of view** (http://www.intelliven.com/subscribe/), apply what they learn, review what happens, review results with advisers, try again, and ultimately manage to incorporate what makes sense and what works into their own approaches to leadership, both now and as their careers unfold.

Follow this link to subscribe to, or follow, intelliven.com in order to join and participate in a community committed to intelligent venture evolution.

Terminology

The word Strategy means different things to different people in different situations. The glossary of strategy terms below provides a consistent foundation for material presented throughout the workbook:

- **Strategy** is what people in an organization plan to do in order to "win" whatever game they are playing.

- **Strategic thinking** is how decisions and actions are made in the immediate-term in a manner that is mindful of long-term implications and consistent with a strategy.

- **Strategic planning** is the structured process that management uses to periodically engage leaders in advancing their strategy.

- **Strategic plan** is a description of an organization as it presently exists, where it is to be in the future, and how it will go from where it is today to where it will be next on the way towards a long-term vision.

- **Strategic initiatives** are projects identified as part of strategic planning and documented in the strategic plan that are to address what is most important to change next in order to increase the odds of winning.

- **Strategic management** is what is done to deliberately operate and develop the organization in a manner that is entirely consistent with its strategy.

---

2 See: The E-Myth Revisited: Why Most Small Businesses Don't Work and What to Do About It Michael E. Gerber (http://www.amazon.com/Michael-E.-Gerber/e/B001I9OR5G/ref=ntt_athr_dp_pel_1): "making pizza vs. making a pizza making business."

Manage to Lead material applies to organizations and leaders. Select an organization to study while using the workbook and prepare to imagine yourself, if you are not already, in the role of its leader. While the material applies to any organization, and even to individuals, learning is enriched if the selected organization meets the following criteria:

- It is of significant scale and complexity, having, for example: over 40 employees, several functional departments, an annual budget of more than $3M, and over five years of existence.

- Select an organization, whether it be your own, where you currently work, an organization in your community, or one where you might like to work, to which you have convenient access to those in charge. You will need to speak with organization leaders as part of completing workbook assignments. (Email your **professor/author** with the name and a description of the organization you have chosen for approval.)

professor/author: peterd@ intelliven.com

Note to OD Students and Practitioners

The application of behavioral psychology to organizations over the past 60 years or so has given rise to Organization Development (OD) tools, methods, and principles. University programs and training labs have taught thousands of professionals in the rapidly evolving discipline. Many of those trained wonder where they ideally fit in the organizations that employ them.

To set the context for thinking about where specially trained resources fit in an organization, consider how other emerging competencies have evolved to fit in organizations. What happened when information technology (IT) entered the work scene provides a case in point.

Stage 1: New competence comes from a source outside the organization. Prior to World War II, IT had yet to enter organizations. When the potential utility of computing power first appeared, organizations hired outside experts (see *Figure 4*) who were specially trained to conceive, design, develop, implement, and support ways for IT to drive value.

Stage 2: New competence brought into the organization in a staff position. After experiencing success with outside resources in the '60s and '70s, organizations realized that they would be able to harness and deploy the benefits of IT more efficiently if they staffed their own organizations with IT competent personnel as indicated in *Figure 5*.

Figure 4. New competence comes from outside the organization.

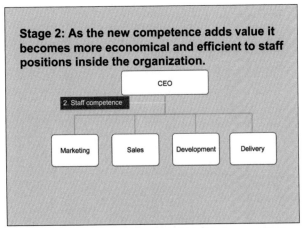

Figure 5. *New competence brought inside to support role.*

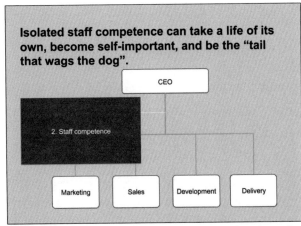

Figure 6. *Support role swells to disproportionate scale.*

IT departments grew in importance in the '80s and '90s as investments in IT improved productivity and performance. In some, if not many or even most, cases IT departments became disproportionately powerful in their own right with relatively large budgets and the power to decide, even over the CEO, what got done in the organization as suggested by the graphic in *Figure 6*.

Stage 3: New competence becomes a core competence across the organization. Gradually, IT competence has filtered into the mainstream such that organizations today are often even run by CEOs with IT competence (see *Figure 7*) and are no longer likely to be held-up by IT politics. Instead, organizations are being defined by their ability to powerfully employ IT.

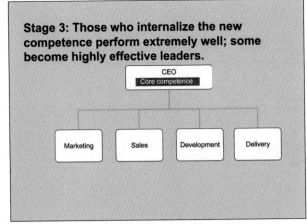

Figure 7. *New competence absorbed into the line.*

IT competence is becoming ubiquitous. Every role in an organization will be carried out better because those in it are able to see and seize the potential to improve performance with the intelligent application of IT (as suggested in *Figure 8*). IT is headed to be like water, electricity, and phone service in that it will be provided by an outside utility and not manufactured and tended to by resources internal to the organization yet everyone will know how to use it and draw on it to help them perform at peak levels.

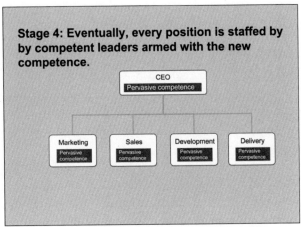

Figure 8. *New competence becomes a core skill.*

OD may be going through a similar progression from outside, to inside staff, to inside core, to pervasive competence in organizations. While the evolution is playing out, those with OD training should either **use OD to help organizations perform better in whatever role they happen to be in or help others in key roles to internalize and effectively use OD** tools, methods, and principles.

The mindset and objective in the latter case, though, ought to be for the OD consultant to put him or herself out of a job. Success for the outside or inside OD consultant is when what s/he knows how to do has been internalized by those s/he helps. S/he can then go on to help others.

That said, OD consultants are a long way from being out of work because it will take decades, if not a century or more, for OD competence to become commonplace. And, in that time, new OD tools, methods, and principles to deploy will certainly evolve to keep OD employment high.

OD professionals who want to secure their financial independence (see *Why Growth is Good and Money Matters* (page 154) in the Appendix) may be wise to consider that those who develop, internalize, adopt, and use OD as a skill in their job function will achieve and be recognized for success and be better rewarded than those who provide OD advice, as important as it might be.

OD competence may eventually show up everywhere in organizations just as today we expect to find rigorous analytical thinking to be universal and ubiquitous across an organization and not housed somewhere in an organization's math or economics department. The evolution of OD competence in-the-line will likely progress through a continuum from unaware to innovator as suggested in *Figure 9*.

In the meantime, those committed to the evolution of OD competence and the improved performance it helps secure, should, regardless of where they sit in the organization:

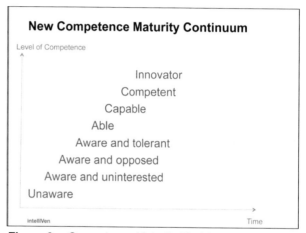

Figure 9. *Competence Maturity Model*

- Look for and capitalize upon opportunities to personally make a big positive impact by applying OD tools, methods, and principles to improve performance. Do NOT lead with OD…lead with the improved performance that OD helps produce.

- Find and help develop those in the organization with potential to understand, internalize, and intelligently use OD tools, methods, and principles to perform better.

- Track and promote successes. Consolidate, model, and communicate lessons learned and best practices.

- Connect with those in other organizations, including universities and labs, to systematically bring in new material and contribute to the field.

When considering the points, work problems, and cases presented in this workbook, **there are always three perspectives to consider:**

- That of an **outside consultant**; an individual practitioner or as an employee or contractor with a small or large consulting firm.

- That of an **inside consultant**, such as one who provides staff support in an Human Resources department.

- That of a **worker** in a functional area, such as in marketing, sales, delivery, development, and accounting, or in the role of unit leader or even CEO.

Use and experience all three perspectives when working with the material especially in the cases, the work problems, and the organization selected to study. If you plan to move on in the role of consultant, remember that one learns to *give* better feedback by first learning to *get* feedback. The same is true for what is taught here in that you will do a better job helping clients to perform and grow if you have first stepped into their shoes and put the tools, methods, and techniques into practice in the role of manager or leader.

The Seven Truths

The seven truths, taken as a whole, are really quite powerful. Some may ask: *"Do I need to be a better manager?"* or *"Do I need to be a better leader?"* The answer is often that it would help to be both a better manager *and* a better leader. Acting in concert with the seven truths allows you to do both by managing better in order to be a better leader. In that sense one really can *Manage to Lead*.

Each truth is simple…some say, "disarmingly simple". Further, the truths apply equally well at any "level of system" which means they apply to:

- An individual trying to do something like, say, get fit or stop smoking.

- A group of people who want to accomplish something important as a team.

- A company trying to enter a new market or roll out a new product.

- A township trying to improve its attractiveness.

- A country campaigning to depose a dictator.

It is in this vein that the truths can be used to help you change the world whatever scope that world happens to have.

There is structure to the truths in that each drives clear and specific action. Each chapter of this workbook covers one of the truths plus the actions it drives and introduces tools and methods to carry out those actions.

Finally, all the truths are present and applicable all of the time. They are not steps or stages and they are not numbered or sequenced. Those who seek to improve their organizations should examine each truth all the time and actively progress towards ever more clarity and maturity of action on the one that gives the biggest lift in performance at that point in time.

Here are the seven truths:

- **An organization exists to solve a problem for people.**
- **It takes a team.**
- **Context matters.**
- **It pays to pay attention.**
- **No leader succeeds alone.**
- **It is OK to do what you are good at and like doing.**
- **Growth is good.**

The following sections unpack each truth in turn and the actions it drives in order to help you change the world in a planned and intended manner.

Each section presents material in prose and in figures. The workbook is designed to be read and used on a personal computer or mobile device with access to the Internet. It can also be used in hardcopy form though some of the material will be inaccessible.

Each section covers one simple truth and the actions it drives with supporting work problems and examples. Activate links to templates, additional reading, and case material to fully explore the potential to understand and apply presented material.

The Appendix presents blog posts from www.intelliven.com that are the most relevant to points covered and that may be particularly useful to those who endeavor to implement some of the suggestions and ideas in their organization or in client organizations.

Truth. An organization exists
to solve a problem for people.

Action.

Get Clear

Know whose problem you solve,
how, and how well.

Get Clear

An organization is a social group which distributes tasks into systems that work together to achieve a collective goal or purpose. The word organization comes from the Greek word *organon,* which comes from the word *ergon* which we know as 'organ' and which means a **compartment for a particular job**.[1]

The simple truth is that the purpose of an organization is to solve a problem for a customer[2] which drives the action to be clear about whose problem the organization solves, how it solves the problem, and how well it solves it.

All businesses and many, if not most or even all, other organizations (such as non-profits, churches, and government agencies) ought to get, and stay, crystal clear about what problem they solve and for whom. It is common for leaders to describe their organizations in terms of one or two, but not all three, dimensions because thinking about the three dimensions of **market**, **problem** and **solution** all at the same time challenges the mind and is hard for most people to do for any length of time.

The graphic in *Figure 10* presents a way to visualize an organization in terms of the **problem** it solves (or why anyone needs what the organization provides), for who (**market**), and how (**solution**).

Click on *Figure 11* to activate a template that can be used for any organization to describe **What solution** it provides for **Who** and **Why; or W-W-W.**

While it may at first seem simple or obvious, it is usually surprisingly difficult for leaders to sort out and agree on how to describe all three dimensions. Employee surveys invariably reveal that the most urgent need across the organization is to get a better handle on: "**Who are we and what do we do?**" which speaks to the importance of completing the exercise and for communicating the results.

Top leaders may themselves be clear about one or two of the three dimensions to their organization but do

Always ask: "What solution do we provide for Whom, and Why?"

- Most people relate well to one or two of the three dimensions.
- It is hard to think in three dimensions.
- If they can think in three dimensions, it is hard to stay there.

Figure 10. *Always ask, "What solution does the organization provide for Whom, and Why?"*

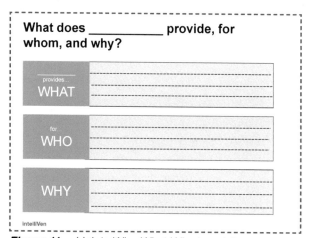

Figure 11. *Link to Who-What-Why template (http://www.intelliven.com/templates/1596-2/)*

---

1 See: http://en.wikipedia.org/wiki/Organization

2 Note that it is commonly attributed to Peter Drucker that the purpose of a business is to create and keep a customer; e.g.: http://www.zdnet.com/blog/collaboration/the-purpose-of-a-business-is-to-create-a-customer-peter-drucker-centenary/1049

not realize that it is critical to be clear about all three. When leaders know and articulate the problem their organization solves for whom, it helps them and everyone else in the organization individually, and collectively, to perform better.

Organizations that have developed a purpose, mission, vision[3], and/or an "elevator pitch" may have already answered the question: "**Whose problem do we solve?**" If not, however, then the mission, vision, and elevator pitch should be revised, or a separate effort undertaken, to clarify the three dimensions.

Most top teams find that it takes several hours over many work sessions over several months up to a year to reach complete agreement on the W-W-W for their organization. It is worth the trouble for those that do because the resultant clarity and alignment pave the way for peak performance.

To illustrate, consider an organization that helps:

- Credit card companies (i.e., the **Market** or **Who**) to

- Increase efficiency of delinquent account collections (i.e., the **Problem** addressed by the solution or **Why** customers are interested in the solution) by hosting a

- Cloud-based automated collection utility (i.e., the **Solution** or **What** is provided).

An organization that has two of the three dimensions the same and a different third might define an entirely different organization. For example, the same cloud-based automated collections system that improves collection efficiency (i.e., the same problem) for a different market (say, state income tax collection departments) might define an entirely different organization because the market served by one organization (credit card companies) is so vastly different than the market served by the other (state income tax collection departments).

Yet another organization might provide a packaged software system that is delivered, installed, run, and maintained in-house rather than a cloud-based solution to address the same problem for the same market. Such a different solution would almost certainly be provided by a different organization because it would be unduly difficult and complex for a single organization to do a good job providing both solutions even though the market and problem are the same as the other.

While varying any one of the three dimensions may define a separate organization, a new organization can also emerge from

---

3 A lot has been written about purpose, mission, and vision so none of these are addressed here. See for example: http://www.skills2lead.com/writing-a-business-mission-statement.html by Jose Luis Romero and Built to Last; by Collins and Porter. This is not to take away from their value; only to note that while important in their own right, if they separately or together do not make crystal clear what problem is solved for whom they are lacking in an important respect.

another. An organization that serves credit card collections departments can expand to focus on state income tax collections departments and/or on telecommunications billing collections and others, for example.

It make sense to set up different organization serve each market because for a single organization to approach and serve more than one market requires a breadth of skills and resources that can be overwhelming to manage. Trying to pursue multiple markets out of one organization would likely cause it to under-perform relative to its potential and relative to its peers.

Where's the data to support need to focus on one market? (biathlete)

EXERCISE 1: ORGANIZATION STUDY

Find the vision and mission statements for your organization and study them carefully to see if the Who-What-Why are easily and unequivocally discernible. Highlight the most relevant portions.

Listen to the background and instructions at this link (**http://american.hosted.panopto.com/Panopto/Pages/Viewer/Default.aspx?id=923396e4-509f-48ef-b6ce-dc100ad29453**). When instructed, stop playback, and click **Figure 12** to read the background on Gap's founding:

Don Fisher, 1928–2009
Gap Inc. Founder

Don and Doris Fisher founded and then transformed a single store in San Francisco stocked with Levi's, records and tapes into a thriving, nearly $15 billion global business with more than 134,000 employees, more than 3,100 stores and a permanent place in pop cultural history. They have been credited with inventing the specialty retail category, though they were equally known for their commitment to philanthropy and civic work.

Throughout his distinguished career, Don kept a sharp focus on growing Gap Inc. thoughtfully, but always maintained a commitment to his family, his philanthropic and civic duties and his love of the arts.

Don had never anticipated that his once small business would grow so rapidly, that it would revolutionize retail and transcend cultures. He'd always envisioned a modest chain of casual wear stores —maybe, as he once put it, "as many as 10." His approach was led by passion and determination—doing things his own way.

The first Gap store, in 1969, would change retail forever.

"Our company continues to demonstrate values that, from the beginning, set us apart— creativity, risk-taking, integrity, loyalty, doing what's right and staying focused on our customers," Don said.

Figure 12. Link to Gap founder history. (http://www.gapinc.com/content/dam/gapincsite/documents/DonFisher_Bio.pdf)

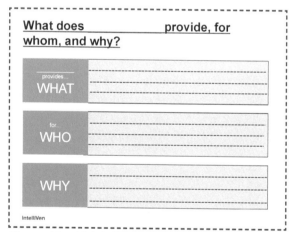

Follow this link (**http://www.intelliven.com/templates/1596-2/**) to enter and submit what problem Gap was set up to solve for whom.

Finish the playback to learn the answer.

Figure 13. Link to Who-What-Why template (http://www.intelliven.com/templates/1596-2/)

Then activate the link in **Figure 13** to enter and submit What-Who-Why for your organization.

Who (Market)

An organization needs customers to serve. Without customers the organization has no reason to exist. The ideal customer, as summarized in *Figure 14*:

Figure 14. *Ideal Customers have five key characteristics.*

- **Has the Problem** the organization solves. There is no point selling a solution for which the prospect has no need. If a prospect does not need the solution because they do not have the problem but do have other problems, organization leaders may be tempted to solve one or more of the other problems. Before proceeding with such a strategy, though, leaders should consider that doing so essentially means building yet another organization defined by a different W-W-W which will drain resources from core activities and add risk and complexity.

- **Finds the Problem Strategic to Solve.** Every prospective customer has many problems but no customer solves all of its problems at the same time. Instead, either explicitly or implicitly, they determine which of all their problems are most important to solve next and allocate resources to solving them. Successful organizations sell their solution to prospects for which it is strategic to solve the problem it addresses.

- **Has Resources.** If the prospect does not have the scope and scale of operations to support paying a fair price for the solution, or if they are otherwise resource constrained say, for example, due to market or economic conditions, it makes no sense to cultivate them as a customer.

- **Can be Reached.** To make a sale requires direct access to the person in the prospective customer organization who will make the decision to allocate resources for the solution. If the buyer cannot be identified or reached the odds of a sale are low no matter how compelling the value proposition.

- **Is Good to Work With.** Some customers are better to work with than others. Cultural differences, regulatory restrictions, complex laws, geographic barriers, and many other obstacles can make some potential customers much more attractive and others less worth the trouble to cultivate.

The above five characteristics of an ideal customer can be used to decide which market segment to sell to next. For example, of all the prospects to sell to next, put a priority on those who have the problem the organization solves, for whom it is strategic to solve it, that have sufficient scope and scale to justify paying a fair price, where the decision maker can be reached, and who is a pleasure to work with. If more than one prospect meets all the criteria, put the priority on the one that offers the most follow-on sales potential.

While the advice above may seem self-evident, it turns out that leaders of most early-stage ventures and of market-expanding efforts inside mature organizations do not follow it. Instead, they almost always sell principally to organizations where there is a key contact that they happen to personally know. That is, they use **Can be Reached** as the primary criteria to determine who to sell to next.

When they run out of sales prospects in their personal network, they then generally set out to make their network bigger by joining clubs, trade groups, community boards, etc. They may get another sale or two but they also get exhausted and eventually learn that a plan to increase sales capacity by extending their network is not a good long-term solution.

Their next step is often to bring on board members and "rain-makers" with deep Rolodexes and who know a lot of people. This may also lead to more sales in the short run but is not an approach that can scale to any significant size.

While using **Can be Reached** as the primary way to decide who to sell to next comes, naturally it is also the least scalable and the easiest of all the ideal characteristics to change. Successful ventures identify who needs to buy their solution because they **Have the Problem** in a big way, it is **Strategic to Solve** it, and they stand to lose the most from not solving it and to gain the most by solving it. That is, the best organizations identify those who come the closest to being the ideal customer and then network directly to those buyers. If needed, they can always find someone who knows, or who otherwise has access to, the target buyer who they can hire or retain on a part-time basis to make the connection.

Why (Problem)

An organization exists to **solve a problem for people**. Organizations seeking to perform and grow are wise to be thoughtful about what problem they choose to solve.

Specifically, as shown in ***Figure 15***, it is easiest for an organization to grow if the problem it solves is **Important, Pervasive**, and **Persistent.** It also helps if the solution addresses a problem that is **Nearby** to other problems and/or that is a **Small part of Bigger Problems**. Finally, the solution needs to drive a price that is **Rational given its Costs** and the **Value** it drives.

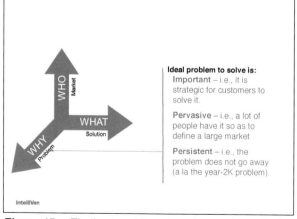

Ideal problem to solve is:
Important – i.e., it is strategic for customers to solve it.

Pervasive – i.e., a lot of people have it so as to define a large market

Persistent – i.e., the problem does not go away (a la the year-2K problem).

Figure 15. *The best problems to solve are Important, Pervasive, and Persistent.*

Every customer likely has many problems but is constrained in how many can be addressed at once by limited resources such as: time, money, and manpower. The best practice is to sort problems in priority order based on the lift in performance that comes with a solution and the drag on performance if not solved.

Resources are then focused almost exclusively on the top few leaving others to be addressed down the road.

Important problems are strategic to solve and get the most time, money, and manpower. If an organization pitches to solve a problem that is strategic, the odds are good that there is a sale to be made. The odds of a sale go way down if the pitch is to solve a problem that is not deemed by the prospect to be strategic.

It facilitates growth further if the problem is **Pervasive**. A pool of potential customers that have the same strategic problem define a market that might be worth going after. A problem that only one customer has might make a good project but will not likely serve well as an engine for growth.

Organizations with solutions to problems that **Persist** are preferred because if the problem goes away, so too will the need for those who solve it! Organizations in the late 1990s that existed to change software systems to work properly past the year 2000 have largely disappeared unless they reframed why they existed to address a persistent problem.

The best problems for an organization to solve also lead to new opportunities. One path to new opportunities emerges if the problem a solution addresses is **Nearby** to other, similar problems that are also important to solve.

A solution that solves a problem nearby to others is represented by the collection of triangles in the lower-right section of *Figure 16*. For example, an organization that provides a system to help with credit collections might find itself in good position to also solve problems near to collections such as credit originations, customer service, and fraud detection all of which have visibility to collections, draw on the same pool of domain and technical expertise, and likely report to the same executive who is the ultimate buyer of such solutions.

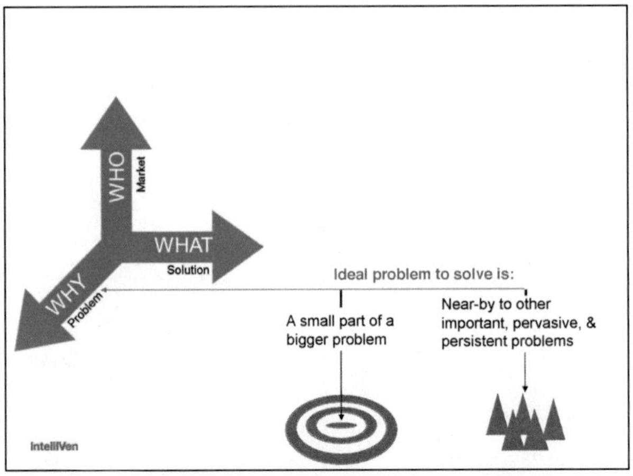

It is ideal if the problem solved happens to be **a small part of a larger problem** that the organization can step-up to also address. For example, as represented by the concentric circles in *Figure 16*, a Credit

Figure 16. *The best problems to solve are nearby to other problems and/or a small part of larger problems.*

Collections System solution sold for $150,000 may serve as the core to a Credit Management (which includes credit origination, servicing, and collections) Solution that sells for $500,000 which itself may be the core of a Retail Risk Management System that has a price tag of over a $1M and which itself may be a part of a $10M Customer Management System. Each solution addresses a broader problem, drives more value, and requires a higher level of budget authority and scope and scale of responsibility to approve.

It is best for an organization to pitch its solution in the broadest possible context but in a way that can be fathomed by the buyer. For example, while it may now be possible to conceive of a $10M Customer Management System it is unlikely that a sale of same could ever have been made if the Collection System had not come before it. In general, a good strategy is to **describe the full scope of potential value** and then sell the **largest small component in the big picture that the buyer can relate to and purchase** based on their present level of thinking, budget authority, scope and scale of responsibility, and experience.

The problem addressed must **justify a solution price high enough to make a fair profit** after covering product development and support, cost of sale, cost of delivery, and general management and administration. It is remarkable how many organizations suffer because their solution has to be priced so low that the revenue it generates barely covers the cost of its sale and delivery.

For example, a Collection System that improves productivity by 85% in a credit department with 110 collectors easily generates enough savings to justify a customer paying $1M over three years based on headcount reduction alone. The same work volume can be completed at 15% of the cost of 110 collectors which cost say, $80K/year, which saves over $7M/year! The market of credit operations with similar scale may be large enough to drive enough revenue using a direct sales approach to support a highly profitable and growing organization for many years.

The same solution probably does not make sense to a credit department that has just a handful of collectors because the savings do not justify the price. If the organization lowers the price, it might lose most if not all of its profit unless it also brings down costs, (perhaps by selling via word of mouth rather than a direct sales approach, delivering the software as a service instead of installing and customizing a version to operate behind each customer's firewall), and if the market is very large. On the other hand, if the organization can find prospects with collection departments that operate with higher headcount, say in the thousands instead of the hundreds, then the price may be too low.

In summary, an organization that wants to perform and grow needs a solution that solves a problem that is:

- **Important, Pervasive**, and **Persistent.**
- **Nearby** to other problems and/or a **Small Part of Larger Problems.**
- **Rational given the costs** of developing, supporting, selling, delivering, and managing it in light of the size of the market that can reasonably be captured and the value customers derive from the solution.

What (Solution)

Every organization provides a product or a service to solve a problem for those it serves. To be chosen by customers to provide the solution it must be better, less expensive, faster, be more expeditiously available than alternatives, or have some other such advantage over alternative solutions. Much has been written to address how to develop a competitive offering and the dimension most organizations sort out well for themselves is their solution. Consequently *Manage to Lead* does not address solutions other than to assume the organization has one that does indeed solve some problem for some specific set of people in a reasonably competitive way.[4]

How (Do-Sell-Grow)

In order to provide solutions to customers an organization needs to develop and deliver its solution, convince customers to use it, and ready itself to develop, deliver, and sell on an ever expanding scale. Imagine an organization that:

- Does not know how it will meet the demands of its current customers.

- Has no idea where its next customer will come from.

- Does not know how it will acquire resources needed to meet an upcoming surge in demand.

Such organizations exist and they are stuck. That is, their ability to perform and grow is severely constrained.

Organizations that experience sustained growth and high-performance *execute, create demand,* and *develop capacity* in orderly, or *systematic,* ways. **A system is a collection of resources working together to accomplish a common goal.** The resources of an organization aggregate into three essential systems:

- The *Execution System,* or what the organization does to **Do** what it does.

- The *Demand Creation System,* or what the organization does to **Sell** what it does, including marketing, lead generation, sales, sales engineering, proposal writing, and sales support.

- The *Capacity Development System,* or what the organization does to **Grow,** including training, recruiting, fund raising, performance assessment, goal setting, systems development, and process engineering.

Anything an organization does other than **Do, Sell,** or **Grow,** makes sense to continue doing only if it facilitates, improves, or otherwise efficiently support its ability to **Do, Sell,** and **Grow**.

---

4 For more on solutions, for example, refer to Competitive Advantage by Michael E. Porter.

An organization that has execution problems essentially has no other problems because there is no point to growing, or to landing new customers, if the organization cannot even **Do** what it does to reliably deliver to customers it already has. Without a way to capture, organize, and distribute its collective knowledge from serving customers, an organization may have a collection of unconnected experiences such that every new customer may be a whole new adventure. An organization that does not know for certain how it will meet delivery obligations runs serious risks and will find it difficult, if not impossible, to maintain control over the quality of its products and services as it grows.

Once there is a reliable way to execute, there is confidence to generate demand. However, without a way to generate demand that is predictable, repeatable, replicable, documented, maintained, taught, and ever-evolving, the organization's ability to **Do** and **Grow** is likely to eventually be constrained by its ability to **Sell**.

When new sales cause demand to exceed delivery capacity, it must **Grow** capacity to deliver. When capacity to deliver exceeds demand, it must **Grow** sales capacity. A growing organization needs to be clear about how it will add capacity to **Do** and how it will add capacity to **Sell**. For many organizations, this means identifying and cultivating sources of people, recruiting, and professional development.

At any time an organization's ability to perform and grow tends to be constrained by one of the three core systems: Do, Sell, or Grow. Leadership's job is to decide which system needs to evolve next and how.

For example, if a product provider generates more demand than can be handled by existing operations, then more delivery capacity is required. Once capacity is in place, sales capacity may need to expand in order to put the increased production capacity to work. However, the amount of sales capacity should likely need to increase at a much slower rate than the rate of delivery capacity because a little more selling capacity should drive the need for a lot more delivery capacity. These dynamics are summarized in *Figure 17*.

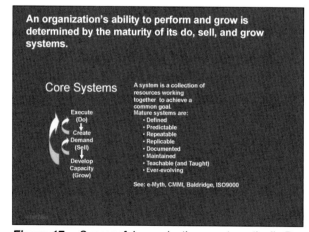

Figure 17. *Successful organizations systematically Do, Sell, and Grow.*

In this sense, then, the evolution of **Do, Sell,** and **Grow** systems is iterative and staggered, with execution out in front of demand creation which is out in front of ability to grow.

The larger and more complex an organization is, the more important it is for it to **Do, Sell,** and **Grow** in ways that are characteristic of more mature organizations; that is the Do, Sell, and Grow systems need to be more:

- defined

- predictable

- repeatable
- replicable
- documented
- maintained
- taught
- revised to reflect lessons learned from experience.

National and international organizations, such as ISO[5], Baldridge[6], and CMMi[7], encourage and help organizations improve the maturity of their systems and processes.

Organizations that experience sustained growth and high performance *execute*, *create demand*, and *develop capacity* in an orderly way. Further, the three core functions are generally repeatable, replicable, scaleable, documented, and systematically taught. They are also proactively enhanced in the face of new techniques, technologies, lessons, and insights.

EXAMPLE

Consider how things work, for example, at an organization that manufactures natural personal care products as illustrated in *Figures 18 and 19*. Rising popular interest in the environment and in responsible consumer care products and ever-expanding technology to work with gives rise to the concept for personal care products made entirely from natural ingredients. The concept for the product evolves and then it must be produced out of raw materials procured in factories.

The amount of the products to make is a function of projected demand. Produced goods are shipped to supermarkets/pharmacies for consumers to purchase. Operations are supported by finance and administration, Human Resources, Learning and Professional Development, Information Technology, and Facilities personnel and governed by the CEO.

List all organization processes and the inside and outside entities they deal with.

- An organization is a system of systems; each of which is a collection of resources working together to: do, sell, or grow the organization.

- Do, sell and grow systems work together to accomplish the organization's purpose which is to solve a specific problem for a specific set of people in a specific way.

- List and connect all entities (people and things) and processes to show what feeds each and what each feeds.

Figure 18. *Example list of entities and flows from a personal hygene products company.*

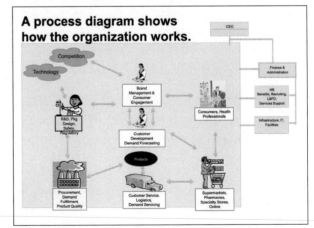

A process diagram shows how the organization works.

Figure 19. *Example of process flows linking entities for a personal hygene products company.*

5 See: http://www.iso.org/iso/iso_9000/.

6 See: http://www.nist.gov/baldrige/.

7 See: http://www.sei.cmu.edu/cmmi/.

How Well

Before deciding how an organization needs to change, it is essential to know how well the organization is performing by selecting performance measures and comparing actual performance to performance goals. Set performance goals based on industry benchmarks for similar organizations at a similar stage of evolution, and doing similar things; performing; and then measuring and comparing results with targets, past performance, and the performance of similar organizations.

This section of *Manage to Lead* presents a basic primer on financial terms and concepts. For some the material presented here may be very basic. For others it may be just what is needed to become familiar enough with basic financial terms so as to not be intimidated by them or by those who work with them for a living.

Three distinct but integrated financial statements tell how well an organization is performing from a financial perspective:

- Income Statement
- Balance Sheet
- Cash Flow Statement.

Each is described in *Figures 20–35* and on the following pages.

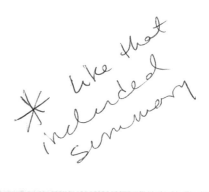

Income Statement

- Revenue

- Cost of Sales or Cost of Goods Sold

- Gross Profit

- Operating Expenses

- Non-Cash Expenses

- Net Income / Net Loss

IntelliVen

Figure 20. *Income Statement*

Income Statement starts with Revenue (or Sales) which is money received for goods and services sold to customers

REVENUE

• Money earned from operations
• Not income from other activities
• Revenue must be earned

Examples of goods and services provided in exchange for revenue:
• Consulting hours
• A report
• Working system
• Facilitated session
• A part
• A product
• Etc.

IntelliVen

Figure 21. Revenue

The direct cost of goods and services sold are subtracted from Revenue to get Gross Profit or Contribution to Profit

REVENUE

COST OF GOODS SOLD
aka COGS: Cost of Sales (COS); costs directly associated with the activities required to earn the revenue

GROSS PROFIT

Example direct costs of goods & services:
• Personnel
• Supplies
• Travel
• Shipping
• Etc.

• Gross Profit = Revenue – COGS

• Gross Profit Margin or Gross Margin = Gross Profit / Revenue

• Gross Profit is the money left to run the business and earn a net profit after meeting revenue obligations

• Negative Gross Profit means costs to earn (deliver) the revenue exceed the (market) price of the good or service

IntelliVen

Figure 22. Cost of Goods Sold and Gross Profit

Example Project Plan

PROJECT PLAN Contract Value: 562,252	Cost/Hour	Actual August	Actual Sept	Actual Oct	Actual Nov	Prjctd Dec	Prjctd Jan	Prjctd Feb	Working View
Revenue		29,068	80,094	163,088	139,020	30,347	70,090	50,545	562,252
Cost of Revenue									
Direct labor		8,300	21,672	35,640	35,746	22,157	19,644	14,166	157,325
Fringe	34%	2,822	7,369	12,118	12,154	7,534	6,679	4,816	53,492
Subs/Contractors				188					188
ODCs					53	100			153
Subtotal		11,122	29,041	47,999	47,900	29,791	26,323	18,982	211,158
ITD Costs		11,122	40,163	88,162	136,062	165,853	192,176	211,158	
Gross Profit		17,946	51,053	115,089	91,120	556	43,767	31,563	351,094
% Revenue		62%	64%	71%	66%	2%	62%	62%	62%
Direct Labor									
Documentation	35				248				248
Front-End Engineer	60			171	189	157	48	40	605
Back-End Engineer	45			432	205	194	208	180	1,219
Quality Assurance	40			60	182	6	48	40	336
Data Base Administrator	50				1		1	1	3
Client Manager	42				2	3			5
Project Manager	72		18	12	17	8	12	8	75
Tech Manager	50		197				5		202
Tech Mgt Support	72		133			54	60	20	267
Total									2,960
Subs/Contractors									
Subcontractor #1	51								
Subcontractor #2	50			2					
Person 3	50								
Person 4	50								

Figure 23. *Example Project Plan*

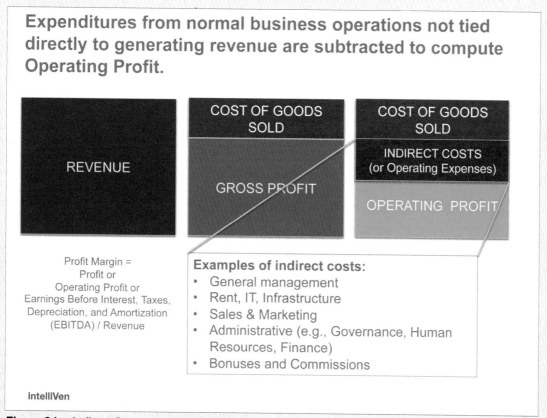

Figure 24. *Indirect Costs and Operating Profit*

Operating Costs

- Operating Costs, Indirect Costs, and Operating Expenses all refer to the costs of supporting direct activities and tend to be organized by function; e.g.:
  - Sales and marketing
  - Research and development (R&D)
  - General and Administrative (G&A)

  to facilitate accountability and external performance benchmarking

- Track labor and non-labor operating costs separately

- Non-cash expenses can be classified as either COGS or operating expenses, depending on use of the asset:
  - Depreciation and Amortization of long-lived assets such as:
    - Equipment (computers, cars, etc.)
    - Software (bought or developed)
    - Facilities
  - Stock based compensation

IntelliVen

Figure 25.   Example Operating Costs

Non-operating Costs are subtracted to get Net Income or, in a non-profit: Contribution to Unrestricted Net Assets.

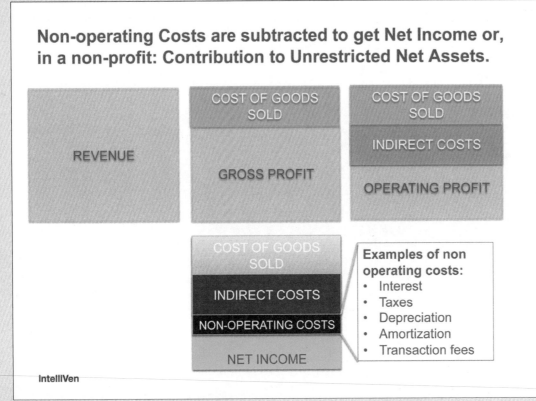

IntelliVen

Figure 26.   Non-Operating Costs and Net Income

Example

Income Statement

	Jan	Feb	Mar	Q1
Revenue	2,873	2,889	3,274	9,037
Cost of Revenue				
Direct labor (DL)	682	776	816	2,274
Fringe on DL	290	318	219	827
ODCs	51	75	86	212
Total Cost of Revenue	1,023	1,169	1,121	3,313
Gross Profit	1,850	1,720	2,153	5,724
% Rev	64%	60%	66%	63%
Operating Expenses	1,074	1,058	1,261	3,393
(Capitalized Development)	(241)	(216)	(220)	(677)
(M&A)		(15)	(74)	(89)
EBITDA (adj.)	1,017	878	1,112	3,008
% Revenue	35%	30%	34%	33%
Amort. & Depreciation	174	167	164	505
Interest, net	160	145	159	464
Income Taxes			698	698
Net Income	**683**	**566**	**91**	**1,340**

Figure 27. Example Profit & Loss Statement

EXERCISE 3: ORGANIZATION STUDY

Review the Profit & Loss statement for your organization.

How is your organization doing in terms of:

- Revenue,

- Gross Margin,

- Profit,

- Profit Margin,

- Employees, and

- Products?

How is your organization doing compared to its performance relative to

- Its annual performance plan?

- Other providers of similar offerings?

- How it performed in prior periods?

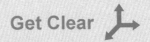

TERMS

Leaders who are in control of their operations compare their organization's actual performance results to:

- Past results-to know whether their organization is trending up, down or level.

- The results other organizations that are doing things similar to theirs achieve-in order to know how well they are doing relative to industry benchmarks, especially relative to those who do best what their organization does.

- Plan, budget, projection and/or forecast-in order to hold themselves accountable to what they said would happen.

- Target or goal-to know if it is time to be done with what they are doing. For example it may be time to prepare to sell and realize gains.

Figure 28 summarizes terms leaders use to talk about their organization's performance with their leadership team and organization stakeholders.

To be in control of operations requires a systematic and programmatic approach to always knowing where things sit.

TERM	DEFINITION	KEY COMPARISON
Target or Goal	How things would ideally be in the long term; i.e., what we ultimately seek to accomplish,	Similar organizations in the same industry
Plan or Budget	How things are supposed to be over a planning horizon (e.g., a year); i.e., what we are supposed to make happen next,	Target; prior period actual results; other players
Projection or Forecast	How things are expected to be in a near-term performance period; e.g., over the next 1 to 3 months; i.e., what we now realistically believe is going to happen next.	Plan; prior period actual results;
Actual	Actual results from a past period; i.e., what has actually already happened.	Past projections; other players; past results; forward projections
Working View	Sum of Actual and Projected results for a planning horizon; i.e., where we now think things will end up for this performance period.	Plan; other players

IntelliVen

Figure 28. Financial Terms

Reforecast is a re-plan when actual and projected results deviate so significantly from plan that it no longer provides management value.

Balance Sheet

Assets are usually at the top
- Current Assets
  - Cash
  - Liquid investments such as money market and mutual funds

- Tangible Fixed Assets
  - Inventory
  - Property, Plant, and Equipment
  - [Accumulated Depreciation]

- Intangible Assets
  - Goodwill
  - [Accumulated Amortization]

IntelliVen

Figure 29. Balance Sheet

Example Assets

BALANCE SHEET

	Jan	Feb	Mar
Cash	7,785	6,686	7,638
Accounts Receivable	12,621	11,428	10,828
Other	193	118	138
Total Current Assets	20,599	18,232	18,604
Fixed Assets @ Cost	3,551	3,551	3,559
Accum. Dep & Amort	(2,996)	(3,020)	(3,046)
Total PP&E, net	555	531	513
Capitalized Software	10,442	10,646	10,871
Deferred Financing	847	847	847
Customer Relations	3,316	3,316	3,316
Accum. Amortization	(7,248)	(7,339)	(7,549)
Trade Names	2,618	2,618	2,618
Goodwill	43,223	43,223	43,223
Deposits/Deferred Tax	268	268	266
Total Other Assets	53,466	53,579	53,592
Total Assets	74,620	72,342	72,709

Figure 30. Example Assets

Balance Sheet

Liabilities

- A liability is a financial obligation, debt, claim, or potential loss

- Short Term (less than 1 year)
  - Accounts Payable
  - Tax Payable

- Long Term (not short term)
  - Notes Payable

IntelliVen

Figure 31. *Example Liabilities*

Balance Sheet

Owner Equity

- What ever is left (positive or negative)

- Total assets minus total liabilities (of an individual, non-profit, or company)

- Assets must exceed liabilities for positive equity

IntelliVen

Figure 32. *Owner Equity*

Example Liabilities & Equity

BALANCE SHEET

Liabilities & Equity	Jan	Feb	Mar
Accounts payable/Accrued	33	144	542
Accrued Payroll/Leave	1,181	1,226	1,253
Accrued Incentives	2,404	99	169
Interest Expense	148	134	148
Deferred taxes	39	39	91
Deferred revenue	5,560	4,790	5,935
Line of Credit			
ST Portion debt	1,500	1,500	245
Other			
Total Current Liabilities	10,865	7,932	8,383
Deferred Taxes	4,162	4,162	5,814
Deferreed Payables	264	268	273
Debt - Senior			
Sub Debt - PIK interest	3,250	3,250	3,250
Debt - Subordinated	12,565	12,565	12,565
Total Other Liabilities	20,241	20,245	21,902
Total Liabilities	31,106	28,177	30,285
Stock	28,550	28,550	28,689
Retained Earnings	14,961	15,552	13,734
Total Equity	43,511	44,102	42,423
Total Liabilities & Equity	**74,617**	**72,279**	**72,708**

Figure 33. *Example Liabilities and Equity*

Cash Flow Statement

- Cash and Profit are NOT!!! the same.
- Important to make sure organization does not run out of cash because cash is as gas to a car… without it things no longer run.
- Links to Income Statement and Balance Sheet.
- Monitored carefully by Lenders, Investors, and CFOs.

IntelliVen

Figure 34. *Cash Flow Statement*

Example Cash Flow Statement

CASH FLOW	Jan	Feb	Mar	Q1
Net Income	683	566	91	1,340
Deprec. & Amortization	174	167	164	505
Deferred Income taxes			(52)	(52)
Changes in Assets/Liabilities				-
Accounts Receivable	(2,961)	1,193	600	(1,168)
Other	65	75	(20)	120
Accounts payable/Accrued	(395)	112	398	115
Accrued Payroll/Leave	48	45	27	120
Acccrued Incentives	54	(2,305)	70	(2,181)
Interest Expense	148	(14)	14	148
Deferred Taxes				-
Deferred Revenue	1,409	(770)	1,148	1,787
Other	9	50	(1)	58
Cash from Operations	(766)	(881)	2,439	792
				-
Capital Expenditures			9	9
Capitalized SW Development	241	216	230	687
Cash Used in Investing	241	216	239	696
				-
Line of Credit, Net				-
Debt principal Payments			(1,255)	(1,255)
Cash from Financing	-	-	(1,255)	(1,255)
Net Change in Cash	(1,008)	(1,098)	951	(1,155)
Beginning Cash	8,792	7,784	6,686	8,792
Ending Cash	7,784	6,686	7,637	7,637

Figure 35. *Example Cash Flow Statement*

EXERCISE 4: ORGANIZATION STUDY

Compile revenue, direct costs, gross margin, indirect costs, and net income for last year, this year (by quarter), next year, and the year after next for your organization.

Compare what you have compiled above to

• prior year performance

• financial plan

• peers

and, in light of the comparison, comment on how well your organization is doing.

Summary

To Get Clear:

- Know whose problem the organization solves.

- Know how the organization: does what it does, creates demand for what it does, and how it grows.

- Know how well the organization does what it does by determining performance metrics and comparing current measures to past performance, the performance of other similar organizations, and to the organization's plan and projections.

WORK PROBLEMS: GET CLEAR

PROBLEM 1. FINANCIALS FOR PROJECT ALPHA

Background:

- Three consultants who earn $50K/year each work full time on project Alpha for an entire year.

- Their work is supervised by a project manager who earns $85K/year and who spends 75% of his time on project Alpha.

- The organization contributes 31% of salary to each employee's benefits (such as social security, personal time off, dental insurance, medical insurance, medical insurance, and 401K).

- The team had $1,000 in taxi costs that were not billed.

- The client paid $650,000 for this work.

Problem:

Calculate Project Alpha's:

- Services Contribution

- Services Contribution Margin

A	Revenue	$650,000
B	ODCs	$1,000
C	Net Services Revenue (A-B)	$649,000
D	Loaded Direct Labor (3*50K+75%*85K)*1.31	$280,013
E	Services Contribution (C-D)	$368,987
F	Services Contribution Margin (E-C)	57%

If you did not get the correct answer please review the financial slides in Figures 20-35 above and try again.

PROBLEM 2. FINANCIALS FOR PROJECT BETA

Background:

- Two developers who earn $59K/year each work full time on Project Beta for an entire year

- 1 subcontractor for whom the firm pays $75K/year also works on the project the entire year

- The work is managed by a manager who earns $85K/year and who spends 75% of her time on Project Beta

- The organization contributes 31% of salary to each employee's benefits

- The team had $1,000 in hardware costs that were not billed

- The client paid $650,000 for this work

Problem:

What is Project Beta's:

- Direct Contribution

- Direct Contribution Margin

A	Revenue	$650,000
B	ODCs (1,000 + 75,000)	$76,000
C	Net Revenue (A-B)	$574,000
D	Loaded Direct Labor ((2*59K + 75%*85K)*1.31)	$238,093
E	Services Contribution (C-D)	$335,907
F	Services Contribution Margin (E-C)	58%

If you did not get the correct answer please review the financial slides in Figures 20-35 above and try again.

PROBLEM 3.

From a financial perspective, which would you rather have: Project Alpha or Project Beta? Why?

- Generally, Alpha is preferred because it has greater contribution even though the margin is a bit lower.

- Other considerations may make a bigger difference; such as which:

  - lead to more revenue later

  - allow us to learn new things that we want to know

  - provide an opportunity to train key staff

If you did not get the correct answer please review the financial slides in Figures 20-35 above and try again.

PROBLEM 4. FINANCIALS FOR PROJEC T GAMMA

Background:

- Same as Project Alpha

- The only other operating costs are:

  - Rent of $15K/year

  - Supplies, equipment and all other non-labor costs of $25K/year

  - A full time administrative support person who earns $33K/year

  - A salesman who earns $80K/year

Problem:

What is the organization's:

- Net Contribution (i.e., Contribution to the organization's EBITDA or Operating Profit)

- Net Contribution Margin

A	Revenue	$650,000
B	ODCs	$1,000
C	NSR (A-B)	$649,000
D	Loaded Direct Labor	$280,013
E	Services Contribution (C-D)	$368,987
J	Services Contribution Margin (E-C)	57%
N	Indirect loaded labor (80+33+25%*85)*1.31	$175,868
O	Non-labor indirect expenses (15+25)	$40,000
P	Total Indirect Costs (N+O)	$215,868
S	Net Contribution (E-P)	$153,119
U	Net Contribution Margin (S/C)	24%

If you did not get the correct answer please review the financial slides in Figures 20-35 above and try again.

PROBLEM 5. DISAPPEARING REVENUE AND CHARITABLE ACTIONS

Assignment:

Read and reflect on the following two cases. Consider from the perspective of:

- The CEO

- An internal OD consultant, or

- An external consultant.

Explain in up to 250-500 words how you would use OD principles, methods, and techniques to address the matter. Prepare to work with those you study or work with to develop further what you come up with.

DISAPPEARING REVENUE

Everything had been going great for your organization when out of the blue 25% of its annual revenue has disappeared literally overnight.

What you would do to help your organization and its leadership, management, and employees deal with what has happened?

- Look for every possible way to improve the situation: raise more from existing revenue sources, cut unnecessary expenses, get better terms from partners, suppliers, and banker; and do it right away.

- Never worry alone. Bring your inner circle together and work on it together.

- Determine what went wrong, why, and what there is to learn from the experience as well as what to do differently going forward in light of lessons learned.

- Have an honest and direct conversation with employees. It may be the time you want to hide … but you need to get out and let everyone know where things really stand, where the opportunity is in this (if it doesn't kill you it will make you stronger). Have a plan to work on it together, rise to the occasion, and pave the way forward.

- Do not sugarcoat reality. Sometimes reality bites! Shrink to size, prepare to grow, and then grow. Get to the right size fast or prepare for death by a thousand cuts (see graphic below).

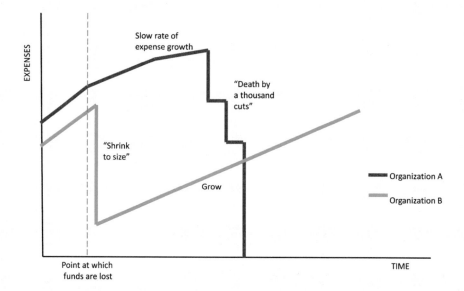

CHARITABLE ACTIONS

Since stepping-in two months ago the CEO has:

- Received a request for this year's contribution to Toys for Tots and the Marine Corp Coat Drive. These are charities the firm has long supported.

- Received notice that a new employee brought on by the CEO wants to invite up to 20 employees to participate in a Hearts and Hammers weekend to help local, low-income home owners fix and repair their residences while building employee community at company expense to cover transportation, meals, supplies, and a few incidentals totaling about $1,750. The new employee has experience with Hearts and Hammers at another firm where it worked well as a bonding experience that did good for the community.

- Been solicited by a personal letter from by a former colleague and good friend, who now heads a like-organization, to buy a table for ten at $2000 to be recognized as a sponsor of a charity ball that will have several prominent current and past diplomats, industry and government leaders, and defense department generals in attendance.

- Been invited to attend a social function at the home of the CEO of a firm the company might like to acquire, to raise funds for children of military personnel who have paid the ultimate price of war and so will not be returning home.

- Been invited by a board member to buy a table for $2500 and to attend his favorite personal charity's annual dinner which raises money to help under-resourced high school students in Washington DC to get on track to attend and pay for college. The board member is the person who the CEO has worked with for over 30 years and who recommended him to the investor that ultimate bought the firm and brought him in to run the firm.

- Been invited to buy a table at the annual dinner of a board member's spouse's non-profit for $3000 which raises money for elderly who are unable to provide for themselves in the final stages of life. The board of the charity is populated by past colleagues of the CEO who would be good to network with. Attending will likely lead to annual requests to attend and recruitment to the board and an obligation/opportunity to serve on its committees.

- Received an invitation (spouse included) from the eldest son of his favorite cousin, who is just starting his career in the same industry, to attend the annual dinner for a non-profit whose board he recently joined. The CEO wants to support his cousin's son's efforts to include socially responsible activities in his life as he launches his career.

- Been informed that a poorly performing executive assistant's home has been victimized by fire and many of the possessions of the four-children, single-parent household are now smoke and water damaged and need to be cleaned or replaced including their carpets and television.

- Received a letter from the local chamber of commerce welcoming the CEO to the new role, their town, and to the upcoming chamber meeting and the $3K annual dues to be a full participating member.

- Received a formal invitation for a free round of golf at the new near-by Presidential Golf Club that costs only $30K per year for company membership that allows 5 named employees to use the club at any time for their personal or business use. As part of playing the round the CEO must bring the CFO and listen to a pitch to accept membership terms over a leisurely lunch.

- Asked to sit on the advisory board of a non-profit organization which helps under-resourced families of children with cancer to cover life costs while parents tend to their sick child (babysitting, gas, laundry, cleaning, etc.). The CEO has served as an advisor to the founder since its inception and helped expand the community of local executives attending the annual dinner from 5 in the first year to 300 in the 4th now with an annual budget of $300,000. Attendees are from firms that are natural allies of the current company as partners, sources of work, sources of employees, and sources of new ideas that drive growth. Participating this year will include serving as event co-chair, making a speech, and buying two tables for guests (which could be recruits, non-government clients, partners, and employees).

- Asked to donate money and technology services, including Web site hosting, of a 5-person (all students at American University) start-up non-profit that the CEO has advised since first meeting the founder and its CEO when she was presented an award for extraordinary achievement at a young age by Jane Goodall, at the Jane Goodall Foundation annual gala two years ago.

- Candidates for local office and their backers (who are prestigious current or former local CEOs of like-companies who are respected, admired, and who the CEO wisely seeks to emulate) asking for corporate and personal donations with the promise to influence key government decisions and to put in place legislation that will be attractive to the firm and its current and prospective employees.

- Seven different Industry associations (TechAmerica, AFFIRM, Professional Services Council, IAC, CEG, NAPA, and BENS) want the CEO and their firm to be a member and consider various leadership roles on their committees and boards.

Something needs to be done soon to decide which of these events to participate in and which to pass on. It takes an enormous amount of time to consider, understand, evaluate, decide, and act on each. It occurs that there may be a way to involve company executives, managers and employees in deciding which to do that may be uplifting to morale, help them learn to work together better across functions, and be expeditious and low cost. The CEO figures they can spend about $15K this year but as the firm grows maybe the amount can increase. Recently, the CEO read an article in Sloan Management Review about Strategic corporate Giving (see below). Maybe there is a way to develop a strategic approach to giving. Clearly this is just the beginning and there will be no end of such requests. What do you do?

- Organize requests into categories and consider on their merits accordingly:

  - Some are marketing expenses

  - Some are corporate development expenses because they lead to better relations with partners and possible acquirers.

  - Some are recruiting expenses

- Develop and implement a policy on political contributions and follow it.

- Set up and drive a cross-functional, cross-level Charitable Actions Committee (CAC) to:

  - Guide organization to support charitable efforts that are connected in important ways to people who work at and that help strengthen the organization's community.

  - Specifically, the CAC will recommend how management should disburse funds it has earmarked for charity and to coordinate the contribution of employee talents and time to activities that benefit local organizations that meet specific criteria the committee develops and recommends for management.

Truth. It takes a team.

Action.

Get Aligned

Decide what kind of leader to be
and collect followers.

Get Aligned

Every organization has, or needs, a leader. And it is true that the power of one committed, clever person can make all the difference in the world. But no one individual, even the greatest leader, does anything of much significance alone. The simple truth is that **it takes a team** to lead an organization. The action motivated by this truth is for the leader to **decide what kind of leader to be and then to attract, collect, and align his/her top team and collect followers.**

The best leaders figure out that it is not all about them. It is about their organizations and the decision to either manage or lead is a false dichotomy. **The one in charge needs to manage in order to lead** and, indeed, can and should *Manage to Lead* his/her organization to achieve the stated vision. **The top person's job starts with managing his/her own self to lead.**

The leader's work is never finished; the job is 24/7 and comes with a ubiquitous, omnipresent, and incessant sense of accountability to owners, investors, lenders, donors, customers, tax-payers, partners, employees and their families, and the local community. The mantel of responsibility is never unyoked and may cause physical distress to those not cut out for the role, or the equivalent of a runner's high to those who are!

The role and specific tasks vary considerably with organization maturity and scale, but the responsibilities presented in *Figure 36* are core to the top job from day-one. Despite the clarity afforded by the list, deciding how to spend time hour-by-hour, day-to-day is far from clear for many, if not most, leaders.

Some leaders wrestle with whether to get work done themselves or to assign and develop others to perform the functions of their organization in an ever-more systematic, teachable, scalable, predictable, and reliable way. As Michael Gerber says[1] it comes down to whether the one in charge wants to "make pizza" or "build a pizza-making business."

What the Leader Decides to Do Matters

When the one person in charge decides to do personally what s/he believes is needed to get work done, no matter how right it seems at the time, s/he should consider the following, all of which can lead to less than optimal results:

---

1 See Michael Gerber, *The e-Myth Revisited.*

LEADER RESPONSIBILITIES

The top person, at every stage of evolution, is expected to:

Set direction, align resources, and motivate action. Said another way, the CEO's job is to: develop, hold , nurture, communicate, and drive to achieve a vision.

Keep the mission, long-term vision, and operating status, relative to performance plans, goals, and objectives, clear and visible to stakeholders inside and outside the organization.

Manage, nurture, and productively employ relationships with outside stakeholders including board members, investors, lenders, partners, donors, advisers, suppliers, community leaders, recruits, and employee families.

Take care of and deploy organization assets (e.g. people, money, knowledge, data, methods, intellectual property, and equipment) in order to maximize the assets' contributions to achieve the best possible results.

Find and develop opportunities for step-function increases in growth, performance, and impact such as new markets, new partnerships, new products, acquisitions, new methods, new systems, and new resources

Identify and drive what is most important to change next.

Do what absolutely has to be done that no one else can possibly do, whether it is to resolve critical operating issues, sweep floors, or plug-in the coffee pot!

Figure 36. *Leader responsibilities*

- Time spent on a specific thing is time that cannot be spent on something that is more important.

- Everyone else in the organization will refrain from doing what the person in charge does for fear of upstaging or competing; their default thinking is that "If the top-dog is doing it, they had better not interfere."

- Others in an organization tend to assume that what the person in charge does is right and correct, so they fail to think critically about it and so tend not to push back when they should.

The net effect is that the most important thing for the top-person to do does not get done, s/he ends up doing what others can and should do, but now avoid doing, and there is a lack of critical thinking which can lead to poor performance. The organization's ability to perform and grow becomes constrained by its top person; and that top person might then wonder if s/he should work on being a better manager, or work on being a better leader.

As suggested by the illustration in **Figure 37**, a leader **sets a direction** represented in the first figure by the target with a bull's-eye in the middle. Then the leader **aligns resources**; that is, the leader collects followers who all look to hit the same target. Then the leader **motivates action**, as suggested by the radio bars in the lower corners of the third figure, which causes the resources to progress towards the target.

The Leader's Job

Set Direction   Align Resources   Motivate Action

Figure 37.   The leader's job The articulation of a leader's role presented in this figure and the next was taught to the author by Fred Nader who is twice past president of NTL and a master OD consultant, facilitator, and team builder.

Another way to say it, as summarized in **Figure 38**, is that a leader develops, holds, nurtures, communicates and drives to achieve a vision. Like Harry Potter and his Marauder's map, the leader holds a map that is always changing, making sense of it, and navigating the course accordingly with the team looking over his/her shoulder.

There are many ways to lead. That is, **there are many ways to behave in the role of leader.**

There is no one right way to lead in all circumstances. A good strategy is to decide how to lead based on the situation at hand.[2] However, consistency and predictability add to the odds of success. It is not a good idea to be one kind of leader one minute and a different kind of leader the next with the same team. Team members value consistency and predictability in their leader so think carefully about what kind of leader to be and then stick with it.

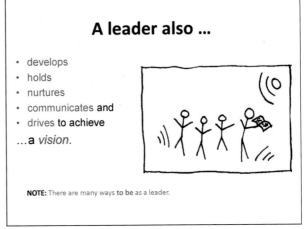

A leader also ...

- develops
- holds
- nurtures
- communicates and
- drives to achieve
...a *vision*.

NOTE: There are many ways to be as a leader.

Figure 38.   A leader holds an ever-evolving map for the team.

---

2 See Ken Blanchard, Situational leadership: http://www.kenblanchard.com/Effective_Leadership_Solutions/One_to_One_Talent_Management/Management_Situational_Leadership_Training/.

WORK PROBLEM 1: GET ALIGNED

Draw a stick figure of a leader in action and share it with classmates or colleagues. Explain the logic behind design elements used in the drawing. Post pictures in on-line or physical work space to share with others. Compare your stick figure of a leader in action with those of the author in *Figures 39 to 44*, all of which he has experienced at different stages of his career.

Figure 39. Sergeant Leader

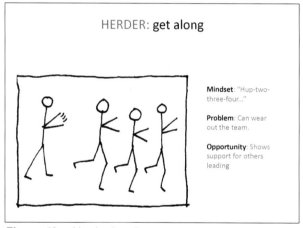

Figure 40. Herder Leader

Figure 41. Icon Leader

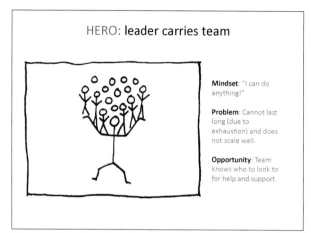

Figure 42. Hero Leader

Figure 43. Teacher Leader

Figure 44. League Leader

Different leadership styles work best given the team's:

- Mission - what is to be accomplished.

- Resources - including who is on the team.

- Timing - how much time is allotted.

- Leader orientation - what the leader is good at and how the leader prefers to work.

Leaders provide the ingredients and ongoing support to what team members do. Great leaders find, attract, recruit, hire and nurture the best and most capable people to develop into the next generation of leaders. Without great people to work with, the leader's own capacity is likely to be the constraint to growth.

Leaders should not be afraid to bring in some who may turn out to be better than they are and/or who are quite different from themselves. The aim is to build a team of complimentary but different skills, views, and orientations to provide a rich environment of diverse thinking and perspectives to work with.

Figure 45. *Six kinds of leaders to choose from*

Top leaders should regularly speak with those they put in charge of organization functions and strategic initiatives about what they are doing; give feedback, coaching, advice, ideas and help assess, problem-solve, plan, and act to make clear what s/he wants done. Look for high-stakes opportunities to personally show what to do in order to produce important results and to allow future leaders to learn from the one at the top.

Constantly and continuously debrief with them in order to consolidate insights based on results and draw out

- What works

- What does not work

- What to do next time.

How to Get Aligned

Wise leaders constantly check with their top team to confirm that they are headed toward the same goals, in the same way, and for the same reasons. The best leaders are always open to input from their top team to tweak goals and plans along the way.

Alignment starts with the leader who is clear about where the organization is headed. If the leader is not clear then no one else can be clear. A leader either:

- Has a **vision and a plan** and is marshaling and motivating resources accordingly, or

- Does not have a vision and plan and is, or should be, **driving to put one together**.

When things fall off track such that the status quo is no longer acceptable the organization will founder until a new vision and plan to achieve it are formed and communicated. To regain its footing a leadership team might go offsite with a facilitator to develop a new vision and game plan.

Preparing for and conducting a facilitated session can accomplish a lot. It can help a leader get clear by serving as a forum in which to talk about ideas and plans; it can help a leader who thinks s/he is clear to **test for alignment** among the top team; and it can inform a leader who is coming up with a vision by getting feedback, ideas, and push-back from those s/he most trusts.

On the other hand, a vision does not magically appear from any facilitated process. Without someone **asserting a vision that is tied to the W-W-W** for the group to react to, work on, and push and pull into something they can all align around, the group will be ineffective. The steps laid out in *Figure 46* summarize the path to alignment.

Many vision-setting exercises get stuck because no one in the group is comfortable enough to put forth a specific idea for fear that:

- Others will think it presumptuous of them.

- It may be ridiculed.

- It may be wrong or inadequate in important ways.

- It may inhibit others with better ideas.

The group though, needs something to work with and it is a leader's job is to give the group that something. **Whoever asserts a vision for the group to work with to a clear conclusion is acting in the role of leader.**

To get a set of possible visions to start with ahead of the session, the leader might do any or all of the following:

- Have each team member submit a vision, anonymously perhaps.

- Hire a consultant to generate alternatives.

- Compile alternatives based on what other admired organizations are doing.

How to Get Aligned

- **Step 1:** Get the leader clear.
- **Step 2:** Get the top team on board.
- Clarity starts with the leader. If the leader is not clear no one can be clear.
- A facilitated session can help:
  - the leader get clear;
  - a leader who thinks they are clear to test for alignment among their top team.
- An intervention can inform a leader who is coming up with a vision but it cannot manufacture the vision for them. You cannot facilitate a vision to hand off to the leader.
- Whoever asserts a vision and then iterates with the team to a clear conclusion is acting in the role of leader.

Figure 46. *How to get the leader and the top team aligned.*

In the session, select one from the above or from what otherwise occurs, and start with that as if it were the vision. Iterate on it until it becomes clear that it is right and alignment can be achieved, or set it aside and work with another. Repeat until a vision to align around is found even if it takes several sessions.

If participants share their thinking openly, fully, and honestly they can go a long way towards achieving the needed clarity. The one who then holds the results of those efforts and who furthers its development, communicates it to stakeholders, and aligns and drives resources in its pursuit is filling the role of leader.

Core Leadership Group

No one leader, and not even any two, has the breadth of competence and depth of capacity to do anything of much significance alone. Successful organizations often have a core leadership team of three to seven top executives who are aligned to accomplish specific goals as a cohesive unit.

The odds of success go way up when the top team has at least three players with different but complementary strengths that are all important to the business and who have:

- Established relationships such that they know and understand each other well and truly enjoy spending time together.

- Extraordinary desire, drive, capacity, and competence to accomplish their goals.

- Instinct and innate drive to work with each other and on what they can do to help the organization to succeed.

- Agreed to give credit for any and all success to everyone else so as to not compromise the odds of success by vying among themselves for credit or praise.

- Drive to grow and empower others over time to behave and perform as they do.

When a core leadership team grows beyond seven in number, successful organizations often find a subgroup, again of three or so, evolves to provide direction and guidance to the entire team.

The inner leadership circle can be called a core leadership group, an executive committee, a steering committee, or any number of other names and is suggested graphically by the three arrows in the figure at the opening of this section. The team of leaders, each with their own

CORE GROUP

team of aligned followers (as illustrated in *Figures 47 and 48*) collectively form a fourth much larger and more powerful arrow headed up-and-to-the-right.

Note that the middle arrow represents the leader and it is no wider than the others because the leader is no bigger or better than anyone else on the team. S/he is just another person playing a key role as are the others.

Keep the concept of the core leadership group low-key so other team members do not stress about whether they are part of the group or not. It is simply a sub-group of leaders who have agreed to keep everything moving in the right direction no matter where they happen to be in terms of organization function, hierarchy, or seniority.

The Core Group meets regularly to keep things on track using an agenda along the following lines:

- Set and manage the leadership team agenda.

- Outline and guide the evolution and adoption of the organization's target mission, vision, culture, strategy, annual plan, policies, and core processes.

- Identify key areas needing attention; assign responsibility and resources and perform governance to be sure they are addressed.

- Set operating priorities.

- Set intent and key parameters to guide core processes (e.g., assignments, incentive compensation, goals, performance appraisals, promotions, salary reviews, staff development, governance, metrics of performance, and communications).

- Prepare and communicate goals, direction and status to the stakeholders including employees, directors, investors, lenders, clients, and partners.

- Consider and act on recommendations from Board of Directors, investors, and advisers including investment decisions.

- Model targeted behavior.

Align leaders for synergy.

Team of leaders — Each leader has aligned followers. — Each leader's team is pulling in the same direction. — Team of aligned teams all pulling in the same direction creates a force to be reckoned with.

Figure 47. *Align leaders for synergy*

Everybody wins.

Leaders of any size organization (20 to 200,000) who get a small group (3 to 7) of strong players all pulling hard in the same direction for an extended period can accomplish nearly anything!

Figure 48. *Aligned leaders are a force multiplier.*

EXERCISE 1: ORGANIZATION STUDY

Use the template pointed to in *Figure 49* to fill out the blue boxes for your organization and to submit it for review:

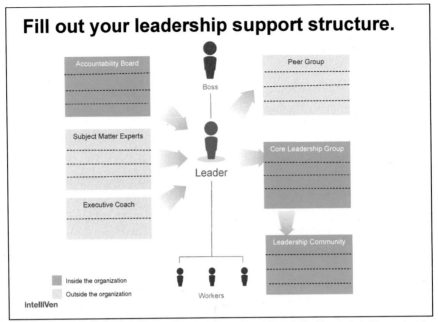

Figure 49. *Link to Core Leadership Group Template (http://www.intelliven.com/templates/leadership-support-structure/)*

Contract and Govern

One of the leader's most important jobs is to get and stay clear about what it is that s/he is counting on from each team member. Once the leader is clear, the message must be communicated to the team member. Often, the leader fails to engage in a rich communication apparently in favor of assuming that team members are somehow supposed to figure out for themselves exactly what is expected.

Click on *Figure 50* to watch a five-minute video of a supervisor and team member making many common mistakes that make it tough for things to come out right:

The following steps make explicit a conversation that otherwise plays-out inside of the heads of those involved. When the conversation is explicit the leader and team member get on the same page and dramatically increase the odds of high-performance and fulfilled expectations.

Figure 50. *An example of what can go wrong with poor contracting.*

CONTRACT

The leader first gets clear about what is needed from each person on the team. For each team member, the leader sets up a one-on-one conversation to relate exactly what the team is counting on from him/her. The leader should be certain that what is said is really what is wanted and that s/he thinks the person is able do what it is the group requires; and then ask the person to repeat back what they were told to be sure s/he has it right; and then ask to verify s/he really does want to do it and that s/he believes s/he has the ability do it.

Once there is agreement between the leader and the team member on **what**, **want**, and **ability**, then there is essentially a verbal contract for the team member to do what is asked. The leader then must ensure that the team member **has the resources** (such as: time, training, people, money, texts, and advisers) needed for success. Finally, the leader must **make it worth the team members while** to succeed (such as by providing praise, a bonus, a promotion, or a trip upon successful completion).

The steps a leader should follow are outlined below in more detail for easy reference:

- Make clear what is to be done. Tell each person and team **what** the team counts on him/her to do; do not assume that just because the leader said it that s/he "gets it", instead:

  - Ask him/her to repeat back **what** was heard to verify it is what is intended.

  - Express confidence that s/he **can** do what is asked.

  - Verify that s/he too believes s/he **can** do what is asked. There is no point in asking someone to do something s/he does not believe s/he can do. Paraphrasing Henry Ford: "*if they think they can or if they think they can't…they are probably right!*"

  - Tell him/her that you really **want** him/her to do what you ask.

  - Verify that s/he indeed **wants** to do it. People often want to do something other than what they like doing and what they are good at doing because they think others value something other than what they are good at and like doing. The leader's job is to make clear that what the team member is good at and likes doing is indeed what is wanted (see Grow section).

  Close out this step by writing down what has been agreed upon and what you will track to know how things are going and to know when what is to be done is indeed done.

Forming

Co - create

- Provide resources necessary to ensure success, such as:
  - Time
  - Space
  - Training
  - Experience
  - Money
  - People
  - Advice
  - Feedback

- Make it worthwhile to succeed; such as:
  - Recognition
  - Admiration
  - Praise
  - Prominence
  - Attention
  - Bonus
  - Trip
  - Award
  - Dinner
  - Raise
  - Promotion

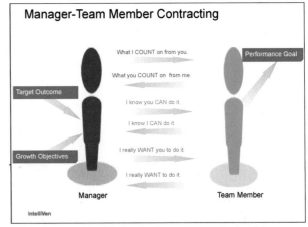

Figure 51. *Contracting between manager and team member*

Figure 51 presents a way to visualize the steps outlined above.

GOVERN

Remember that delegation is not the same thing as abdication and that the number-one reason things go wrong is lack of management attention. The wise leader checks-in from time to time to be sure front-line action is proceeding as expected. Remember that delegation does not mean abdication and that the number-one reason things go wrong is lack of management attention. The wise leader checks-in from time to time to be sure front-line action is proceeding as expected. Go out of the way to make it clear that you are on his/her team and that your only interest is success. Give something tangible to manifest your commitment such as your best thinking in the form of notes or drawings, key insights or ideas and invite your direct report to internalize your input and take it further as though it were their own.

Leaders should set regular (e.g., weekly, bi-weekly) time to talk for 90-minutes one-on-one with each direct report. Schedule in a time-slot that is easy to keep; e.g., 7:30 a.m. every other Monday. Keep the time

more often than not. Reschedule if necessary but commit to it. It is OK if takes less time than scheduled. Any savings will be much welcome found-time. Have no other agenda and do not meet over lunch; though lunches together are good to have.

The team member prepares and presents to their leader in up to one hour:

- Last period's priorities and progress with metrics to support claims of progress; the leader's mindset is to ask: how is it going; how do you know?

- List and talk through the top three to five, but no more, priority items fully to cover: what is going on and how it is going. The leader should go out of his/her way to be supportive, on the same team as the direct report and to help by providing resources, training, head start, access to other people, etc.

- Agree on top items, next steps, what is to be done next and what the leader will do to help.

Weekly Feedback Session

The leader also prepares and presents to the team member in less than 15 minutes:

- His/her top three to five priorities to be kept honest; to let the team member in on something special and on what the leader is doing for the good of the team; and it is good for the leader to consolidate and share such information.

- The leader discusses points raised until it is certain that they are clear and then solicits input and advice.

- The leader commits to follow up to keep the team member aware of what the leader is doing as desired.

Finally, review items for upcoming team meeting (ten minutes); recap and wrap-up (five minutes).

Figure 52 presents a way to visualize the steps outlined above:

Failure to follow the governing steps above can lead to calamity as suggested by the leader who is reviewing a team-member's work in the video presented in *Figure 53*.

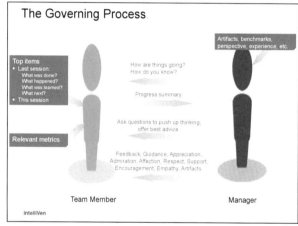

Figure 52. *Govern for success*

Top Team Role Clarity

The CEO of a successful organization ensures that their inner circle of leaders, or Core Leadership Team, are individually and collectively clear about their relative strengths and on what the group counts on from each to be successful. The exercise below is a structured and straightforward way to

Figure 53. *Example of what can go wrong with poor governance.*

make expectations explicit and to open channels of communication between them that can be used to provide each other with advice, guidance, feedback and support in a way that is efficient, edifying, and empowering to all involved.

WORK PROBLEM 2–3: GET ALIGNED

PROBLEM 2 : EXECUTIVE ROLE CLARITY

Preparation

Ask executive team members to read the Get Loose, Get Clear, and Get Aligned sections of Manage to Lead.

At a regularly scheduled executive offsite meeting, dedicate three hours or so before the first break for the exercise described below.

Set up

Ask each executive to print their name at the top of a sheet of newsprint laying on a table or hanging on the wall. Under their name have them write the following headings:.

- At the top: **Good at:**

- 1/3 from the top: **What we count on from you:**

- 1/2 way from the top: **Best Advice:**

Data collection

Ask each executive to move to the sheet to their right and fill in each of the three sections for the person whose name appears at the top. When everyone has finished writing, repeat the previous step until each is back standing at the page with their name on it as in *Figure 54*. Add additional newsprint if more space is needed.

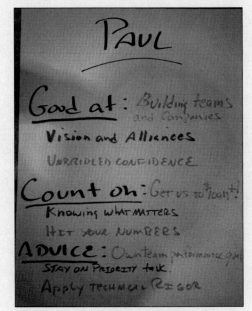

Figure 54. *Sample Role Clarity Worksheet from an executive offsite.*

Process

Ask everyone to read carefully what is written under his/her name in the **Good at:** section; ask them:

- What clarifying questions do you have?

- Do you agree that you are good at the things noted?

- Are there other things you are good at that are missing?

- Are there things you are surprised to see listed?

Ask each person in-turn to read out-loud what is written for them and answer the questions above. Discuss what is said with the group until clarity is achieved and then move on to the next person until everyone has had a turn.

WORK PROBLEMS: GET ALIGNED, CONTINUED

Ask everyone to read carefully what is written under their name in the **Count on** section; ask them:

- Any clarifying questions or comments?

- Do you agree that listed items are your responsibility?

- Is anything you are responsible for missing?

- Do any of your items conflict with each other or with what is listed for others?

- Are things listed consistent with what you are good at such that you can be successful doing them and such that your organization is getting highest-and-best use from you and your talents?

Ask each person in turn to read out-loud what is written for them and address the questions above. Discuss until clarity is achieved and then move on to the next person until everyone has had a turn.

Ask everyone to read carefully what is written under **Best advice**. For one executive, ask them to select one **Best advice** item and have them:

- Ask for clarification or explanation about what is meant by what is written.

- Work hard to draw out what others have to say.

- Not to be defensive in any way.

- Repeat back what they hear to be sure they got it right. Iterate with the group until they are clear and until the group knows they are clear about what is being said and until all agree it is time to move on.

Repeat the previous step for the next person in the group. When everyone has gone start again with the first person and their next item and repeat until all items have been covered for each person.

Ask the group to discuss:

- What they noticed in this exercise?

- What they individually, and as a group, learned about their roles and the roles of others.

- What was learned about how much they have to share with each other and how to do so?

Ask if a similar exercise should be done from time to time with their group and perhaps with other groups in which they work.

Wrap up

A fundamental human need is to be known and understood by others. The first two steps in this exercise help each group member to feel known and understood by those on their team which creates the opportunity for a rich flow of information between them.

The third step builds on and takes advantage of the comfort established in the first two. The result is a deep sense of closeness and connectedness which allows each member of the group to share openly with the others and to be aggressively interested in what others have to say to them. Group members are thus able and inclined to help each other fulfill their potential individually and collectively in the press of day-to-day activity and not just at an offsite.

The exercise can and should be repeated from time to time to keep leaders synchronized and aligned.

The best team members will follow suit with similar exercises with their own teams. The odds of success with this exercise are dramatically improved when it is facilitated by a trained Organization Development professional.

WORK PROBLEMS: GET ALIGNED, CONTINUED

PROBLEM 3: THE OVERRUN CTO

The CEO was brought in by one of the world's most prestigious investment companies to work with the management team of a $15M, 100-person firm with 23% EBITDA margins with the explicit mission to double its size, increase profitability to the mid 30% range, and sell in five years to generate a 3-4X return on their $20M investment while paying down $30M in debt. Everything has to go well to pull this off.

> **EBITDA:** Earnings Before Interest, Taxes, Depreciation, and Amortization.

Five Days after taking the helm of the 23-year old organization, its venerable 36-year old CTO who is the person around whom the firm is built comes to see the CEO at the point of tears and says that she feels it may be best for her to quit and move on to another company because the new 34-year old COO (who created the opportunity for a change in ownership) is inserting himself in work matters that everyone knows are her purview even though the new COO is not the least bit technical (though he is an engineer with an MBA). She says this is embarrassing, disempowering, and that she may just not be needed in the new era.

You cannot afford to lose the CTO. What do you do?

- Below is a list of common answers:

  - Comfort the CTO; express sympathy.

  - Meet separately with the COO and the CTO to draw them each out and to figure out a good solution.

  - Bring the COO in and meet with them both now.

  - Meet with both later.

  - Gather more information.

  - Tell the COO to shape up.

  - Tell the CTO that you really need her.

  - Tell the COO and CTO more clearly what you expect from each of them.

- There are several problems with most of the common answers:

  - Puts the onus for a solution at the feet of the leader.

  - Temptation is for leader to step in to drive, broker, or otherwise provide a solution as it makes him/her feel powerful, useful, important.

  - Risk that COO and CTO become dependent upon the CEO.

- Another approach is to:

  - Offer a tissue to the CTO but do not mention tears; consider them data to suggest that the situation is very serious and indicate anger (see this link on the subject: http://t.co/4cXj5X3u).

  - Ask the CTO if she has expressed her concerns directly to the COO. Likely she has not. Encourage her to do so. Explain that she is facing a significant opportunity to grow as an executive and that it would be a shame to miss out on it.

  - When she leaves your office, immediately call or go see the COO to advise him that it is imperative he hear out the CTO and work out clear roles and responsibilities between them.

  - Follow up with each and both together to be sure they have sorted out who is responsible for what going forward and that they are working well together.

Summary

Decide where to take the organization over what time frame, what kind of leader to be based on the mission, timing, resources, and personal preferences.

Form a core group of leaders with complementary skills and compatible orientations.

Collect followers.

Determine who to count on for what and then contract explicitly with each.

Meet regularly with each direct report to govern for success following the outline presented in *Figure 55*.

The one in charge provides the ingredients and ongoing support to what their operating leaders are doing

- Find, attract, recruit, hire and nurture the best and most capable people you possibly can, to develop into the next generation of leaders.
    - Without good people the leader's own capacity will become the constraint to growth.
    - Don't be afraid to bring in some who may turn out to be better than you and/or who are quite different than you are.
    - Seek to build a team of complimentary but different skills, views, and orientations to provide a rich environment of diverse thinking and perspectives to work with.
- Regularly talk with leaders about what they are doing; make it a habit to give
    - Feedback, coaching, advice, ideas
    - Help assess, problem-solve, plan, act
    to make clear what you want done.
- Look for high-stakes opportunities to personally show what you want done in order to produce important results and to allow future leaders to learn from you.
- Constantly and continuously debrief with them in order to consolidate insights based on results and draw out
    - What works
    - What does not work
    - What you want done next time.

IntelliVen

Figure 55.   *Recipe for managing direct reports for success.*

Truth. Context Matters.

Action.

Plan Change

Decide what must change,
why, and how.

Plan Change

Over time, organizations perform at some level. After start-up, things fall into place leading to a period of rapid growth. The rate of growth eventually slows and then plateaus perhaps due to new technology that spawns competition or maybe due to the organization slowing down in the face of its increased scope, scale, and complexity of operations.

At any point along the way there are always three choices (as depicted in *Figure 56*):

- One is to keep doing things the way they have always been done. Most of the time, keeping things the same is the right answer because to do otherwise means constant change which leads to chaos. On the other hand, **if an organization always only does that which it has done to be successful up to now someone or something will eventually overtake and possibly bury it.** One-product organizations such as some that sold buggy whips, record players, and video rentals are examples of those that rode a wave to oblivion.

- A second option is to change a little which can improve things for a while but if an organization only ever changes at the margin it runs the risk of creeping incrementalism and eventually it too might fade away. A recent example of an organization which may be suffering from creeping incrementalism is the Canadian firm Research in Motion which makes the BlackBerry.

- The third choice is breakthrough change to reach an entirely new level of improved performance where the cycle starts anew. Apple is a good example with its introduction of new products and entire product lines; IBM is also a good example in that it makes more money now from providing services than it does from hardware even though they still go by the name IBM (where the M stands for Machines) and will likely never change to IBS (where the S stands for Services)!

Successful organizations have one step-function improvement after another (as suggested in *Figures 57 to 59*[1]) and leadership's job is always to determine what is most important to next change and do differently.

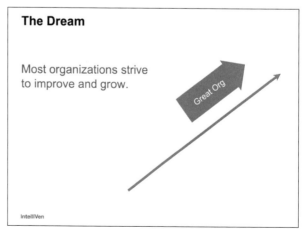

Turbulence requires action.
There are three choices of action in the face of growth and changing internal and/or external circumstances.

No change: Most of the time, no change is the right answer; constant change would be chaos and could be disastrous.

Change a little: Always changing only a little leads to "creeping incrementalism" and eventual vulnerability.

Change a lot: From time to time you need to change a lot because if you always do only what you have done to be successful up to now, you will surely fail (eventually).

GROWTH

TRANSFORM

TURBULENCE

DEATH SPIRAL

IntelliVen

Figure 56. *Link to a summary description of three choices in the face of change. (http://www.showme.com/ sh/?h=N78hmCG).* Adapted from Catlin & Cookman Group's Building the Profit Spiral ®

The Dream

Most organizations strive to improve and grow.

Great Org

IntelliVen

Figure 57. *The dream for every organization: steady growth over time.*

---

1 Adapted from Catlin & Cookman Group's Building the Profit Spiral ®.

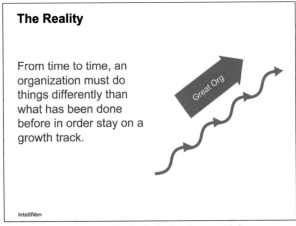

Figure 58. *The reality is that steady growth is interrupted by bumps along the way.*

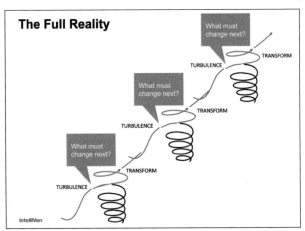

Figure 59. *The full reality is that long-term success requires breaking through to new levels of performance over time.* Adapted from Catlin & Cookman Group's Building the Profit Spiral ®

Find What to Change Next.

If the leader thinks s/he knows what needs to change and that everyone is aligned, ask: "**How do you know your team knows what you want to do**; why don't we ask them just to verify? If they all say what you expect them to say, a positive step towards getting what you want done will have been taken just by bringing it to the center of their attention. If it turns out that some or all of the team are not as aligned as expected, then remedial steps can be taken."

Survey the leader's top team and ask each:

- To describe the **current state**, that is: how things are today.

- **What really good things happen if we change and what really bad things happen if we do not?**

- To describe **how things would be in the future** if their ideal changes were successfully implemented.

- **What needs to be done** in order to get from where things are today to where things would ideally be next?

- **What will make it hard** to do what needs to be done in order to get from today to the targeted next state?

Review results with the leader to bring him/her up to speed on the group's data. Look for and discuss fully any points the leader finds confusing or surprising.

Convene an offsite with the leader and the leadership team to review collected data, reach consensus on each of the five topics, and decide what needs to be done. At the offsite, review survey responses one question at a time in the order above. Highlight responses that are the same or similar thereby indicating progress towards consensus. Guide the group to discuss the data until agreement is reached on how things are today, why things need to change, and **how things would be if the desired change had been implemented.**

The Change Framework

The diagram in *Figure 60* presents a convenient way to visualize and store the group's consensus in a **Change Framework** diagram similar to that originally introduced by Richard Beckhard and Wendy Pritchard in Changing the Essence: The Art of Creating and Leading Fundamental Change in Organizations, Jossey-Bas Inc., San Francisco, 1992 (http://www. amazon.com/Changing-Essence-Fundamental-Organizations-non-Franchise/dp/1555424120).

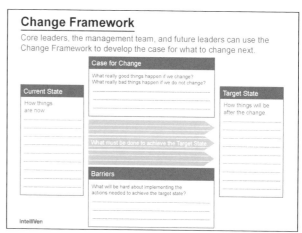

Fill out the Change Framework (http://www.intelliven. com/templates/change-framework/) to make a clear and compelling case for each initiative. Iterate with the team until all members are crystal clear about each initiative.

Figure 60. *Use the Change Framework to make the case for each Strategic Initiative.*

If participants share their thinking openly, fully, and honestly they can go a long way towards achieving clarity and alignment. An effective leader then holds the results of these efforts and furthers their development, communicates progress to stakeholders, and assigns, aligns and drives resources in their pursuit.

A well formulated initiative, using the **Change Framework**, tells a story about **where things are, why they need to change, how things would be if the intended change occurred and what must be done to get from here to there**. A well-crafted change framework is rational, compelling, and flows smoothly from the present through to the future.

Follow the tips in *Figure 61* to piece together the context and the story for each of the initiatives the organization must do next to stay on track to long-term growth and performance.

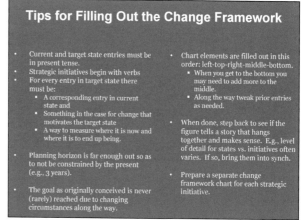

Figure 61. *Follow the above tips to build a clear and compelling case for the change driven by each initiative.*

Enrollment

Many management off-sites produce a list of initiatives, such as shown in *Figure-62*, after intense effort and exhilarating breakthroughs. A list without context, though, fails to reveal the motivation and importance behind each initiative and so makes it difficult to communicate or to muster the energy, resources, and commitment beyond the session needed to implement them.

Using the **Change Framework** instead of a simple list helps but even still, far too often, the same initiatives are again listed at the next offsite with little if any progress since last time simply because no one was put in charge and resources never allocated to implement them.

INITIATIVES SUMMARY

	STRATEGIC INITIATIVES	OPERATIONAL INITIATIVES
EXTERNAL (Mary)	1. Communications 2. Fundraising 3. Strategic Data Collection, Analysis, & Strategy Development Support 4. Default Strategy for the Board	Manage and develop external and government affairs, Board, partners, brand, and community support.
OPERATIONS (Mark)	5. Georgetown Managed Growth 6. Information Technology	Develop hospital-by-hospital operations strategy and conduct plan reviews to develop an integrated view of all operations (administrative, financial, clinical, and capital asset management).
FINANCE (Joe)	7. Capital Asset Acquisition Plan (Facilities Assessment)	Develop hospital-by-hospital financial strategy and conduct plan reviews to develop an integrated view of current state and path to targeted financials.
MEDICAL AFFAIRS (Anya)	8. Oncology Integration	Develop hospital-by-hospital and collective clinical integration strategy and conduct plan reviews to identify strategic opportunities for integrating clinical services across the system.

Figure 62. **Initiatives Summary** *A classic looking list of initiatives from an executive off-site.*

Upon reaching agreement, the group may feel drained but good about what it has accomplished. It is important to make sure the group knows it has done great work and come a long way **but there is still more important work to be done.** Their effort may be for naught unless one more step is taken.

Initiative-to-Action

After the list of initiatives is developed and before ending the session the leader assigns each team member to:

- Take 20-minutes to **fill out an Initiative-to-Action template** using the link in *Figure 63*, for a specific initiative, preferably one the leader would like the team member to sponsor.

- **Lead the group in a brief discussion** about the assigned initiative.

Each team member, in turn, briefs the group on their initiative using the filled out Initiative-to-Action form. As each speaks, the rest of the leadership team adopts the mindset of close adviser and on the same team as the one speaking. Their objective is to ensure that the key points from the group's work are captured so that the best thinking of the group is at-hand and in mind as efforts to progress with the initiative proceed on the heels of the session.

Filling out and briefing the **Initiative-to-Action** form launches the governance process and gets a leadership team member into the role of the initiative's executive sponsor and on-the-hook to make progress on behalf of the group. As such the team member

Figure 63. *Click on the figure to fill out and submit the Initiative-to-Action form for a Strategic Initiative. (http://www.intelliven.com/templates/initiative-to-action/)*

becomes accountable to the group for progress on their initiative. Motivation and commitment soar and the odds of making progress go up as well. Over the ensuing performance period, the leader calls on each team member at some point to brief the group on how their initiative is progressing.

CHANGE FRAMEWORK

Leaders used the Change Framework to determine what to change next to go from **functional to cross functional teams**.

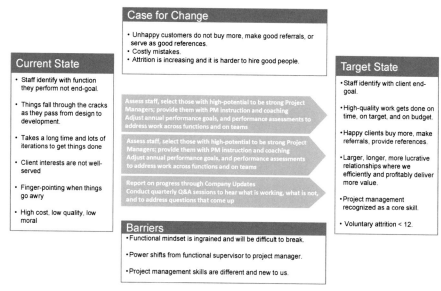

Example Change Framework for an organization whose leaders decided to move from a functional to a cross-functional approach to client services

Summary

Leaders decide what is most important to do *differently next*. Be mindful about what to change and just how crucial it is for the organization. Be interested in and open to ideas for change that come from within the organization and not just from the top.

Use the Change Framework to lay out the foundation for the business case behind every Strategic Initiative. Make sure there is a tight linkage between current state, case for change, and future state for every change initiative.

Context matters. Before launching a change initiative know:

- Where things are now.

- Why things must change.

- Where things would ideally be next.

- What must be done to get from where things are to where things need to be next.

- Why it might be hard to go from current to future state.

Think through how each initiative requires change in **systems,** change in **processes,** and change in the **organization.** Be sure that each sort of change (i.e., system, process, and organization) has a its own plan to communicate how it will be accomplished; resources assigned to ensure it is; metrics to track progress along the way and to know when targeted goals have been achieved, and governed to monitor and track progress.

Have executives fill out and brief the Initiative-to-Action template for one or two initiatives before completing an offsite session in order to start implementing and governing initiatives right then and there when the energy and enthusiasm are high.

EXERCISE 1: ORGANIZATION STUDY

Fill out and submit the change framework at this link for your organization. (http://www.intelliven.com/templates/change-framework/)

Prepare a ten-minute pitch with up to five visuals (posters, slides, or handouts.) that you would make to the CEO of your organization to address his /her and his/her organization's needs.

Present your pitch to the CEO or to someone assuming the CEO's role. Permit others to observe you so doing. Debrief with the CEO and observers what worked well, what happened that was interesting, and what could have gone better.

Reconvene with a team to factor in input from the CEO and observers to revise your pitch.

Pitch the CEO, or a surrogate, a second time.

Note what happens. What went well, what was interesting, and what could have been done better?

EXERCISE 2: ORGANIZATION STUDY

Click on the Initiative-to-Action template (http://www.intelliven.com/templates/initiative-to-action/) and fill out and submit the form for one of the top strategic initiatives you imagine your organization leaders would have listed at their annual planning executive offsite.

WORK PROBLEMS: PLAN CHANGE

UTILIZATION MATTERS– PART A

Background

- $50M business application software firm based in Vancouver, CN with major offices in London, Melbourne, South Africa, and Chile.

- Customers are those responsible for mine safety and supplies at the world's largest precious metal mining companies . Software helps design safer mine support structures and organizes flow of supplies for optimum safety and efficiency.

- Owned by a Private Equity firm keen for the firm to offer professional services in addition to software; significant demand for help using the software to operate mines better and more safely exists based on what the competition offers.

- The firm has no experience selling services and is off to a rocky start in that staff that could be providing services is available, there is work for them to do but yet they charge their time to product support rather than client work.

- The top execs from headquarters, each regional office, and each function meet every six months for three days to work on the business. The most recent meeting was in Chile at which you facilitated an all-day session on how their initiative to grow professional services is going.

Fill out Change Framework and Initiative-to-Action form for the circled initiative in **Figure 64**.

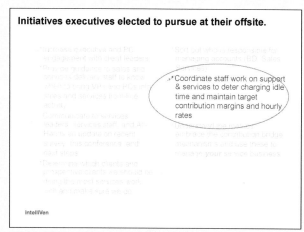

Initiatives executives elected to pursue at their offsite.

*Coordinate staff work on support & services to deter charging idle time and maintain target contribution margins and hourly rates

IntelliVen

Figure 64. *Utilization Matters - Part A*

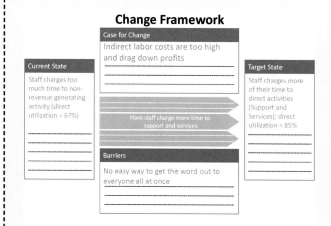

Change Framework

Case for Change
Indirect labor costs are too high and drag down profits

Current State
Staff charges too much time to non-revenue generating activity (direct utilization = 67%)

Have staff charge more time to support and services

Target State
Staff charges more of their time to direct activities (Support and Services); direct utilization = 85%

Barriers
No easy way to get the word out to everyone all at once

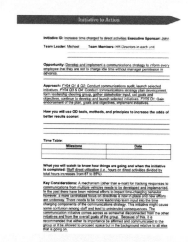

Truth. It pays to pay attention.

Action.

Do & Review

Take action.
Review what happens.

Do & Review

When top leaders are informed, thinking critically, and engaged enough to provide guidance and direction, things tend to go pretty well. That is, things get done better, sooner, and more smoothly when leaders pay close attention. This section describes an efficient way for top leaders to get and stay up-to-speed, see and understand what is going on, ask questions and think critically, develop a point-of-view, and to provide advice and guidance on their organization's most important functions, projects, and initiatives.

Nearly all of the things that cause activities and initiatives to go off track could be averted if someone in a position of authority had been involved enough to give guidance along the way. It is hard, though, for leaders to stay sufficiently engaged even in the most important activities and initiatives because it takes time and focused attention that are routinely diverted to other urgent matters.

There are a lot of reasons why a given activity or initiative might be considered important. For example, it may be relatively large; risky; involve skills and methods that are new to the organization; have potential for great leverage in terms of intellectual property development, revenue generation, cost savings, or skill development. When an activity or initiative is important, it is also important that the effort stay on budget, on time, and on target!

The best way to ensure on budget, on time, and on target performance is for top leaders to regularly review with those responsible for completing the activity or initiative, how things are going. Doing so provides an opportunity for:

- Activity and initiative leaders to step back from the press of day-to-day in order to pull together a consolidated picture of what they are doing to share with others in a safe environment: to challenge thinking, get advice and counsel on strategy, focus, and next steps, and to receive guidance, ideas, and access to resources that can be brought to bear so as to increase the odds of success.

- Executives to stay in touch with what is going on with front-line activity. Any important activity (e.g., delivery, sales, development, marketing, and strategic initiatives) should be reviewed regularly to keep leaders informed about what is going on and for leaders to efficiently provide guidance and direction, consolidate insights across activities, and to drive cross-sharing of resources, insights, and ideas in the best interest of the organization as a whole.

As suggested in *Figure 65*, informal communication on progress is not enough. Neither are occasional one-on-one chats. It is important that those in charge prepare to brief others on their efforts in a scheduled forum where the activity or initiative is the only agenda. Even better is when leaders from across and outside the organization with a stake in performance, intimate affiliation with the organization, or with relevant past experience and knowledge, also attend.[1]

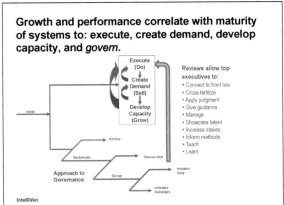

Figure 65. *Summary of approach to governance.*

Leaders set the tone for reviews to ensure that they serve their intended purpose and that they are not done just for the sake of it and to be sure they do not become a "dog-and-pony" exercise. Reviewers must make it safe for those whose work is being discussed to embrace the process and seek input from participants because what is being reviewed *is* what the organization does and deserves input from the best the organization has to offer.

A review is an efficient and smart way for leaders to keep close to what is really going on and to increase the odds that important work gets done well. Reviewers must not look to find fault or assign blame. Instead, they strive to understand what is really going on and to find the best way to improve performance and learn the most.

Reviews also:

- Provide visibility for key staff.

- Create high-stakes circumstances that pushes up performance.

- Create a forum for executives to model the behavior they want others to emulate.

- Reveal important lessons and insights to share with other teams and initiatives.

Reviews are considered successful when:

- The leader of what is being reviewed and the leader's team:

  - Have stepped back from the press of the usual day-to-day to pull together what they are doing into a consolidated whole and shared it with supportive professionals who themselves have reviewed advance materials, showed up, paid attention, participated, and supported the team by challenging its thinking, offering best advice, and provided access to outside resources that can be helpful (such as written materials, outside experts, training, and time that will help improve performance).

---

1 Hrebiniak's Making Strategy Work presents a comprehensive approach to ensuring project success reviews

- Are confident that the preparation process, the review meeting itself, and the follow-up will help them achieve project objectives better, faster, and more smoothly.

• Management is enlightened with respect to what was reviewed; specifically, what is working, what is not, and what needs to be done and learned as a result.

• The organization's best ideas, thinking, resources, and skills have been brought to bear.

• Participants know that

- They are supported, appreciated, enlightened, engaged, heard, and respected.

- Appropriate next steps have been lined up in the face of the realities and understanding reached.

• The leader of what is being reviewed understands and internalizes:

- The group's best thinking in terms of what can be done to most improve performance and/or lower risk and is committed to making that happen.

- The top few actions necessary to follow through.

- What others will specifically do to support these efforts.

• An open discussion of status leads to the fertilization of ideas across the organization.

• Top leaders collaborate in support of the front-line team's efforts and keep from doing the team's work for them.

• The work is completed successfully or is going so well that reviews are no longer necessary to ensure success!

Eight Reasons Management Review Meetings Underperform

The main reason things go wrong is lack of management attention. Hence the importance of management reviews! However, management reviews can also go wrong. Here are eight reasons why they often do:

8. *The leaders did not prepare, so the meeting becomes the preparation and the review never materializes.*

7. *Too much time spent on history, storytelling, and showboating. It is up to the leaders to be sure that whatever is really important gets covered.*

6. *The leaders talk right up to the end of the meeting and never created a space for the reviewers to ask questions, clarify, challenge, and then offer their best thinking.*

5. *Top management fails to create a safe environment thus turning the review into a sham (a.k.a. dog-and-pony show).*

4. *Management fails to really pay attention to see what needs to be seen and to deal with what needs to be dealt with rather than seeing what they want or hope to see.*

3. *Management fails to generalize what is learned to incorporate and reuse elsewhere*

2. *Management discovers during the review that things are in much worse shape than expected and, without intention, makes the management team feel inept by piling on and trying to help too much in the moment.*

1. *The number one reason why these meetings do not go well is that the most important reviewers fail to show up due to last minute crises or they show up physically but not mentally.*

WORK PROBLEMS: DO & REVIEW

UTILIZATION MATTERS – PART B

Review (as presented in this slide):

- What this initiative was to accomplish

- What was done

- What happened

Assume the role of initiative leader and prepare to brief executives about the above as well as on:

- What you learned

- What you plan to do next

Present what you prepared to a review panel.

Initiative was to: Get staff to charge their time to **Support & Services** activities instead of to **Idle** while maintaining target contribution margins and hourly rates.

- **What was done:**
  - Announced goal to increase time spent on direct activities to 61%.
  - Staff was told to charge time to direct activities (**Support** or **Services**) and not to overhead (**Idle**).

- **What happened:**
  - Staff charged time to **Support & Services** even when not actually doing support or services work.
  - Contribution margins [(Revenue-Direct Costs)/Revenue] dropped precipitously:
    - Support went from 70% to 55%
    - Services went from 55% to 49%

- What do you learn from this?

- What you plan to do next?

- What could explain observed results?

IntelliVen

What was learned:

- Telling staff to charge to support activities caused them to do exactly as asked and it led to higher cost of labor with no increase in revenue which drove gross margin down.

- Time charged to direct may not have been appropriate.

What could explain observed results:

- Too many staff on hand; i.e., not enough work for number of staff on board.

- Staff not aggressively seeking work to do once current assignment completed.

- Management not pushing work to staff.

- Amount of time it takes to do the work is underestimated based on industry benchmarks.

- Staff working too slowly relative to industry benchmarks (lazy, not trained).

- Client needs are going unmet.

- Additional clients needs could be developed.

What is planned to be done next:

- Clarify that goal is to improve utilization with no Gross Margin degradation.

- Inform staff to only charge time to support if time is actually spent on legitimate support activities.

- Motivate employees to get themselves charging direct.

- Make it a performance goal for supervisors to get their staff billable.

- Find more billable work for staff.

- Right-size staff level.

Measure and Control

It is impossible to control what you **cannot**, and what you **do not**, measure. For every important thing that the organization does, decide what is most important to monitor and then watch carefully to know how things are going.

A measurement requires a number, as opposed to a sense or a feeling, that is directly related to the subject at hand. Chosen measures are monitored continuously relative to plan.

If you do not know what to monitor then:

- Watch everything you can think of and whittle away what turns out to not be useful and keep watching what does turn out to be useful.

- Study similar organizations to learn what they track.

- Look up industry analysts and market researchers to find out what they watch.

Set targets for chosen metrics based on what similar, ideally the best, organizations do. For example, if sales and marketing expenses combined total 15% of revenue for the best organizations that do something similar then use that as a benchmark (i.e., a point of comparison). Note that it is OK to have a different target as long as there is sensible justification.

Prior to any given period of performance, predict how what is about to happen will show up in the targeted measures. Then perform and monitor what happens. Compare actual measured results with what was predicted. The shorthand for this process is: **Predict-Perform-Measure**.

Study what happened to determine why what actually happened varied from predicted results. Learn from the experience and then decide what to do differently going forward. The shorthand for this process is: **What-Why-So What-Now What?**

The process chart in *Figure 66* shows the measure and control sequence starting in the upper-left with defining overall success and moving down to the lower-left to determine what to watch based on what others who do something similar watch. Next, in the lower-left, the leader predicts what will happen upon performance. Then the organization performs, measures, and compares actual results to projected as suggested along the diagonal to the upper-right. If actual results are in-line with projection then all is well and the cycle is repeated.

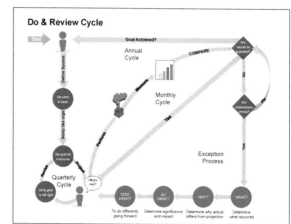

Figure 66. *Do & Review Cycle: What-Why-So What-Now What?*

When actual results differ from what was projected, analyze what has happened after making sure measurements are correct, to move from the upper-right to the lower-right.

Moving from the lower-right along the bottom back to the lower-left in **Figure 66** are four key questions:

- What happened?
- Why is what happened different than what was projected to happen?
- What is learned from this?
- What will be done differently going forward as a result of what has been learned?

Appropriate changes are implemented and the entire process is then repeated over and over until desired results are achieved and the goal is reached.

According to Kotter, who studied thousands of organization initiatives, there are eight reasons why initiatives fail to achieve their intended goals, as summarized in **Figure 67**. If management pays enough attention along the way then none of Kotter's reasons need come to pass! To that point, Capers Jones in the early 1990's conducted a study that showed over 90% of initiatives fail due to lack of management attention. That is to say, whichever of Kotter's eight steps is about to doom an initiative can be averted if management has an eye on things and guides appropriately in the face of reality.

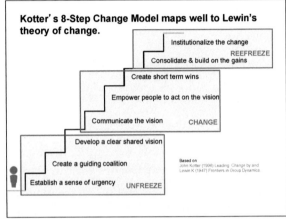

Figure 67. Kotter's eight step model compares well to Lewin's theory of change.

High-stakes Behavior Change.

One way to get people to behave differently than they are used to behaving is to **tell** them what to do and expect them to **do** it (as suggested by *Figure 68*). This model has been used successfully by military organizations' for thousands of years. It is a proven approach for managing life-and-death situations where clear accountability and instant certainty of action are critical. However, in organizations seeking to foster innovation and growth, it is extremely constraining.

Figure 68. The mandate approach to changing behavior.

Clearly communicating target behavior is a good first step but just doing so is not likely to induce the desired result when those effected find the change **abrupt, hard to understand**, and **hard to internalize.** In such cases they may, instead, be likely to keep doing what they have always done.

The odds of change adoption increase significantly when those effected learn and understand the **reasons** for the change *in addition* to the target behavior. Once the reasons are clear, each person effected is in position to **internalize** and **embrace** the change and so make the decision to intentionally **act** in accord with it (as suggested by *Figure 69*).

When a critical mass of those affected understand **what** they are supposed to do and **why** they are supposed to do it, the odds increase that they will also decide that they **want** to do it and then that they take initiative to go out of their way to **act** in a manner that is consistent with the intended behavior as similarly captured in and old Chinese proverb:

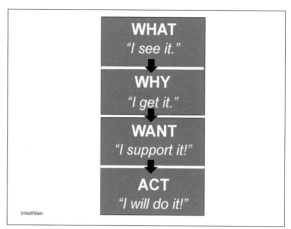

Figure 69. *Enlightened approach to changing behavior.*

Tell me and I will forget.

Show me and I will remember.

Involve me and I will understand.

Step back and I will act.

Govern

The initiative leader applies him/herself to the task of doing what s/he said they would do and then, after an interval, prepares for an **Executive Session** to discuss:

- What s/he said s/he would **do.**
- What was actually **done.**
- What **happened.**
- What has been **learned** so far.
- What s/he plans to do **next.**

Reviewers **ask questions to push-up thinking** and offer **best advice**. The process is then repeated as long as value is added or until the initiative goal is achieved.

Scheduling reviews motivates quality effort; no one wants to show up more than once without having honestly tried to do what s/he said at the prior session would be done by the next session.

Meet Regularly

An organization that knows how to run and use meetings well can improve the odds of achieving maximum performance. On the other hand, it is easy for an organization to lose itself to an endless series of bad meetings. This section addresses the three stages of a good meeting, meeting roles, and how to increase the odds of a successful meeting by putting together and driving to implement a good meeting plan.

MEETING STAGES

All meetings occur in three sequential stages: the ramp-up to the meeting, the meeting itself, and the follow-up to the meeting. Successful meetings begin well before they start and end well after they are over. Specifically, a meeting begins when it is first conceived and its planning starts.

The Ramp-Up gets meeting stakeholders involved so that when the meeting starts they hit the ground running. The idea is to bring to the forefront of their thinking matters which will be covered in the meeting so that they walk-in prepared, with a point of view, and ready to participate and not just wing-it, work on-the-fly, or off-the-cuff.

Figure 70 shows a way to visualize the three meeting stages. The area on the left represents the Ramp-up to the meeting. The oval in the center represents the Meeting itself where the top of the diagram is the beginning and the bottom is the end of the meeting. The area on the right depicts the Follow-up stage and suggests what happens after the meeting.

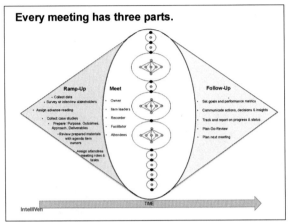

Figure 70. *Every meeting has three parts.*

To bring attendees "into the room" ahead of the meeting, the Meeting Owner with help from their Facilitator (see meeting roles below) may:

• Send the agenda and advance reading materials to those who will attend in order to give them the chance to read, think, develop points of view, and generally get ready to participate. They may not read all of what is sent but it will be their choice and if most do prepare then that will become the norm and those who do not prepare will look foolish.

• Review material in draft, as it is being prepared, with agenda-item owners to be sure they are on target. The odds of having a great meeting and of achieving superior results go way up when the meeting owner sits down with each of those who have speaking roles ahead of the meeting to make sure each item is on track to achieve desired results, push-up performance, and determine how to impact, guide, and use what is coming to maximum affect.

• Distribute the POAD (see below) and invite meeting attendees to comment on agenda items, suggest additional items, and share their thinking on key topics; this gets people to feel a sense of worth, ownership, and concern for the meeting and its purpose to increase the odds that they will internalize the meeting's importance, decide they want the meeting to go well, and take positive steps towards helping to achieve targeted results.

Many meetings are recurring. A series of meetings on the same subject, with excellent preparation, facilitation, and follow-through can be an effective way to make a lot of progress on a specific agenda; such as managing a business, a unit, a product, a client, a project, an initiative, or a functional area (e.g., sales, marketing, or development).

Figure 71 graphically depicts such a series of meetings on a single subject such as product status meetings, a monthly Managers Meeting, quarterly Client Account reviews, weekly Strategic Initiative reviews, Policy Committee meetings, and All Hands meetings.

The idea is to see each meeting not as an isolated event but as integral to building on the one before and feeding the next. In this way a series of meetings provides a solid foundation for governance to ensure top performance on any aspect of operations.

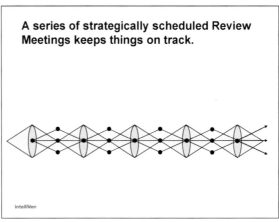

A series of strategically scheduled Review Meetings keeps things on track.

intelliVen

Figure 71. *A series of well-run meetings provides a platform for continuous improvement.*

MEETING ROLES

Below is a list of key roles in most meetings. Sometimes the same person fills more than one role. For example, the Scheduler might also be the meeting Owner. Some roles cannot be effectively performed by the same person; for example, it is virtually impossible for the same person to simultaneously do a good job in the roles of Owner, Facilitator, and Recorder.

- **Owner:** The person who decided to have the meeting and who is the primary author of the meeting's Purpose, Outcomes, Approach, and Deliverables and who is responsible for its agenda, content, handouts, and for publishing meeting record upon completion.

- **Scheduler:** The person who schedules the meeting to accommodate those who are required to attend, readies the meeting room with space, seats, equipment, refreshments, and provides other administrative support as required.

- **Facilitator:** The person who works with the meeting owner to understand their goals and to make sure they are met. Toward that end, the facilitator keeps the meeting on track and on time and reviews and enforces agreed upon ground rules.

- **Recorder:** Records action items, key insights, decisions, and matters deferred for another time on a shared display (e.g. on a white board, newsprint, overhead, or large post-it sheet) for all to see as they are consolidated in the meeting and distributes in draft after the meeting and helps the meeting owner consolidate input to finalize and distribute.

- **Required Attendees:** The people invited to the meeting who must attend. If they cannot attend then the meeting needs to be rescheduled so that they can. Some may have the job to prepare and present material in the meeting.

- **Optional Attendees:** Those invited to the meeting who can attend if they want to and are able to, but the meeting will proceed even if they are not present.

- **Monitor:** The attendee assigned to track and processes individual and group behavior relative to agreed-upon meeting ground rules (see below).

Ultimately every attendee must know why s/he is to attend and what is expected of them.

MEETING PLAN (POAD)

The meeting owner, often with the help of a trained facilitator, a trusted close-in adviser, or one or two of the key attendees, thinks through and documents fully the meeting's Purpose, Outcomes, Approach, and Deliverables, or POAD for short. Every meeting worth having has a plan that addresses its POAD. Prepare and publish a document that fleshes out each section.

You dramatically improve the odds of getting what you want when you are clear about what you want. A POAD makes clear what you want from a meeting and so dramatically increases the odds that you will get it. Once the POAD is prepared, it is a matter of orchestration to achieve meeting success. See **Executive Session POAD** for an example in the Appendix.

Purpose : The Purpose section of the POAD explains why the meeting is to be held so that attendees understand the reason for their attendance as individuals and as a group. Completes this sentence with as much specificity as possible:

The purpose of the meeting is to...

Purpose Examples	The following examples finish the sentence above:
	• ...decide whether to include post-award deliverables in Vendor internet Portal.
	• ...review plans and progress towards developing more business at the Department of Homeland Security.
	• ...review the progress towards completing assigned tasks on the CitiBank installation to identify risks and mitigation strategies
	• ...determine what is most important to change next to maintain targeted growth trajectory.

Outcomes : Targeted outcomes can be hard or soft. Hard outcomes are things you can see or touch such as a decision, a document, or a list. Soft outcomes might be feelings or thoughts, such as leaving a meeting feeling energized. To define targeted outcomes, answer this question:

At end of the meeting what needs to occur for it to have been time well spent?

- Make sure meeting outcomes are aligned with organization goals.

- Limit list of outcomes to three to five.

- Display outcomes for all to see, debate, and refine.

Hard Outcome Examples	• Design specifications for a new feature of our product. • A list of things we want to keep the same in our organization. • A chart showing who at NASA we want to talk to about what in order to get on track to delivering more value there. • A chart showing who at a known new prospect we need to talk to in order to be sure they understand ways to increase productivity in their operation and where we fit in.
Soft Outcome Examples	• Participants leave feeling energized. • Meeting owner feels supported by their team and by management. • Management is assured that their assigned team is on track to complete their work on time, on target, and on budget.

Approach : The steps that a meeting goes through to accomplish its Purpose and to achieve its Outcomes. The approach includes the agenda which plays out in the meeting but it also includes what is done ahead of the meeting and afterwards to ensure success.

Each element of the approach has a link to the purpose, an outcome, and/or a deliverable, someone who is assigned to make sure that its goals are met, a topic, leader, beginning and ending time, and related materials.

A well-planned agenda:

- Balances high-energy topics with those that are more intense.

- Allows time for thoughtful discussion.

- Includes breaks when meetings run over long periods.

- Makes clear how attendees are to think about the item; specifically is it to provide information or is it to generate input or to reach a decision.

Deliverables : Good meetings produce something specific that is fed back into the organization so that operations are enhanced in some way; such as:

- Clarity as to who executive team members count on for what.

- A decision as to who to promote.

- A list of important calls to make to existing clients and associated scripted messages.

- Who at a key prospect will be spoken with by whom about what, how, and when.

- A design approach to implement a key new feature.

Meeting Tips[2]

- In all meeting phases, insist that everyone involved behave in a manner that is entirely consistent with the way leaders want everyone in the organization to behave all the time. By so doing, meetings provide an active forum in which to model target behaviors so as to accelerate an organization's cultural evolution in in specific ways.

- Open with a check-in including an ice-breaker to get attendees "in the room" and to get comfortable with each other.

- Agree on a signal to invite participation such as raising a hand or turning a name-plate on end.

- Agree on another signal to point out ground-rules violations.

- Arrive before the meeting starts and end after it is over to take full advantage of important interactions that take place in those moments.

- Begin on time even if everyone is not present as a sign of respect for those who arrive on time, and to reinforce to latecomers the importance of punctuality. Agree on a penalty (e.g., a fine) for those who arrive late.

- End on time. Even better is to end a few minutes early. Attendees will appreciate the additional minute or two to decompress and compare notes and arrange follow-up interactions with fellow attendees.

- If a meeting is scheduled to occur at meal time provide food or advise attendees ahead of time to bring their own, eat ahead, plan to hold off until afterwards.

- The meeting Owner and the Facilitator should monitor the meetings' progress to determine if its Purpose and Outcomes are on track to being achieved and to drive to stay on schedule towards that end or, if necessary, tweak what is going on even possibly preempting the agenda in order to accomplish the most important goals.

Open the Meeting

At the start, the meeting Owner, with the Facilitator, should:

- Welcome Attendees and thank them for coming.

- Introduce the Recorder and Facilitator.

- Review the agenda. Be sure Attendees understand what is coming and give them a chance to ask questions and propose last minute upgrades.

- Review the targeted Outcomes.

- The Owner starts the meeting but does not dominate it.

---

2 For more on how to run a great meeting, see: How to Make Meetings Work (http://www.amazon.com/exec/obidos/tg/detail/-/0515090484/qid=1126793161/sr=8-1/ref=pd_bbs_1/102-7994389-6513702?v=glance&s=books&n=507846), by Michael Doyle and David Straus.

Guide Meeting

- If the meeting is one of a series, set the context, summarize the work of previous meetings, and review the status of key action items, results, and impacts.

- Keep discussion focused on planned agenda items. Use a "parking lot" on a shared-display (i.e., on newsprint or on a whiteboard) to record topics or comments not on agenda for later processing.

- Look to the Facilitator to make adjustments if conversation gets off track or loses steam and to watch the clock and keep on schedule.

- Ask attendees how to handle unexpected circumstances and needs such as breaking from the agenda or overrunning the meeting end time.

- Agree how to handle bathroom breaks; for example, will there be scheduled breaks or should individuals take a break when needed with as little disruption as possible.

GROUND RULES

At the beginning of each meeting, the facilitator asks the group to agree on and commit to follow meeting ground-rules. Add or adjust rules as appropriate to give power and ownership to the group and to accommodate special circumstances. Appoint an attendee to monitor performance relative to the ground-rules. If a rule violation occurs, agree on whether and how the monitor should intervene; e.g., by flashing a signal (for example, holding up a yellow or a red card).

If the Monitor fails to intervene when a violation occurs, the group brings it to the Monitor's attention and asks him/her to follow the agreement. If the Monitor does not agree or consistently fails to perform the function, the role should be reassigned. If a single person gets more than three exceptions, they may be asked to leave the meeting. If s/he fails to leave, the meeting may be adjourned at the discretion of the group and or the meeting Owner.

The scheme to use a Monitor works well because it is usually much easier for participants to address the Monitor for not jumping in than it is for them to give feedback directly to an offender when a rule is violated. In this way, the entire group efficiently works together to routinely follow the rules.

High-performing organizations act intentionally. Meetings are an ideal forum in which to both articulate and model target behavior. Meeting Owners on their own, with their core leadership team, and with help from a trained facilitator if available, develop three to six ground-rules to review with attendees.

Each rule is consistent with how the leader wants people to behave in meetings and in general. When introduced for the first time, read each rule aloud and encourage discussion to be sure it and the reason for it, are clear and to get the group's buy-in. Also to encourage clarity and buy-in, adjust the rule as needed in response to input from the group.

Too many ground rules or ground-rules that are complex can be overwhelming so keep the list short and the rules simple. Start with just a few that seem most appropriate and add others as needed and as the group becomes comfortable developing, managing and using its rules. Drop rules that become second nature and that no longer need to be called-out in favor of those that need to be added to next shape behavior.

Ground rules persist from meeting to meeting so there is no need to develop new ground rules for each meeting. It is a good practice to have both ground-rules that are used at all meetings and a few that are specific to whatever a given group is working on next.

Review ground rules to open each meeting to remind attendees how they should work with each other. Meeting Owners should walk through all ground-rules for new attendees ahead of, or at the start of, their first meeting.

Procedure: On a whiteboard or on posted newsprint or poster paper, list ground rules in lettering large enough for everyone in the meeting to easily read. At the beginning of each meeting, until they are all second nature, the Meeting Owner or Facilitator, asks the group to agree on, and commit to follow, posted ground-rules. Add or adjust rules as appropriate to give power and ownership to the group and to accommodate special circumstances.

CLOSE THE MEETING

Consider the following guidelines when closing the meeting:

- End on time and on a positive note.
- Thank attendees for coming and for their participation.
- Invite the Recorder to review his/her notes aloud to capture the best thinking of the group before breaking up.
- Review actions and assignments and time to complete.
- Set the time and date for the next meeting.
- Set expectations as to when the meeting record will be distributed in draft and then in final form.
- Agree on how Attendees will talk about the meeting with others in the organization.

GROUND RULES TO CHOOSE FROM:

- Act as part of collective leadership vs. representative of a constituency
- Everyone participates, no one dominate.
- Stay mentally and physically present.
- One person speaks at a time; no side conversations.
- Start and end on time.
- Work the point, not the person.
- Commit random acts of kindness.
- Stay on point; avoid long-winded stories and irrelevant detail.
- Pay attention, show respect.
- Say what is on your mind IN the meeting not afterwards.
- Seek first to understand.
- Show up on time.
- Come prepared.
- Be insightful and supportive. Think before speaking.
- Deal with the real issues; avoid seeing only what you want to see.
- Summarize, consolidate, and crystallize key insights to share with others.
- Recognize the positive and celebrate success.
- Respect confidentiality; if sensitive matters are shared, they stay in the room.
- No storytelling.
- No grandstanding.
- Challenge others in a positive way.
- Stay until after the meeting ends.

MEETING RECORD

The Owner works with the Recorder to compile during the meeting and to edit and distribute finalized meeting notes to the Attendees within a few days using the **Meeting Record Template (http://www.intelliven.com/wp-content/uploads/2012/03/Meeting-Record-Template.doc)**. Note that the meeting record does not need to include who said what but does need to record key decisions, insights, and action items reached and agreed to in the meeting.

There really is "***power in the pen***". The person who takes notes and then drafts and distributes the Meeting Record is demonstrating leadership. Deciding how what happened in a meeting is to be memorialized is a power move. Powerful leaders own and drive the process to produce the Meeting Record. It can be an inclusive process guided by the leader as long as what is recorded turns out to be accurate and forthright.

Every meeting has three kinds of outputs: Action Items, Insights, and Decisions. It does not matter so much who said what and when they said it. What matters is what all those in attendance agreed to along these three dimensions.

The Meeting Owner should designate someone to serve as the official note-taker at the start of the meeting. During the meeting everyone helps the appointed note-taker to keep track of Action Items, Insights, and Decisions as they occur. The note-taker reviews with attendees what they have noted just before adjourning. Upgrades are offered and duly noted.

Within 36 hours; that is before the "forgetting curve" kicks in, the Meeting Record should be drafted by the designated note-taker and reviewed and upgraded by the Meeting Owner. The Meeting Record should then be distributed in draft form to all attendees who each check their own notes and recollections to suggest upgrades. The note-taker and Meeting Owner consolidate and reconcile any and all input to arrive at a final record that is distributed and filed for future reference.

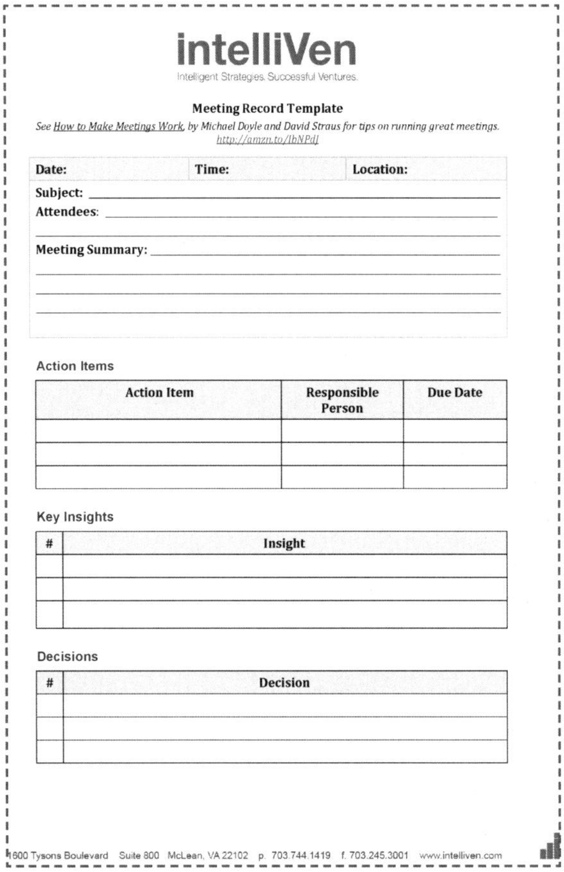
intelliVen

Intelligent Strategies. Successful Ventures.

Meeting Record Template

See How to Make Meetings Work, by Michael Doyle and David Straus for tips on running great meetings.
http://amzn.to/IbNPdJ

Date:	**Time:**	**Location:**

Subject: ______

Attendees: ______

Meeting Summary: ______

Action Items

Action Item	Responsible Person	Due Date

Key Insights

#	Insight

Decisions

#	Decision

1600 Tysons Boulevard Suite 800 McLean, VA 22102 p. 703.744.1419 f. 703.245.3001 www.intelliven.com

Figure 72. *Link to Meeting Record template. (http://www.intelliven.com/note-on-meeting-records/)*

Encourage attendees to consider the draft record carefully and to weigh-in on points that should be refined, added, or deleted by email directly to the Meeting Owner and Recorder. Reply All can also be used as long as input is consistent with meeting content and not the equivalent of a newly dropped bomb.

Figure 72 provides a link to a Meeting Record Template.

Summary

Every important thing an organization does should be subject to a continuous and rigorous Do & Review cycle for the organization to learn, grow, and perform up to its potential.

Apply the Measure and Control learning model to everything the organization does to:

- Do
- Sell
- Grow.

Compare and explain projected and actual results to:

- What others (especially the best) do.
- What the organization has done previously.
- What was supposed to happen according to plan and projection.

The virtues of Do & Review apply to every level of system (e.g., person, team, unit, organization, community, or even country) and in all time-spans (e.g., monthly, quarterly, or annually). Review everything important that the organization does.

Keep and post a schedule of upcoming reviews.

Ensure consistent attendance by a diverse group of knowledgeable stakeholders.

Construct a POAD for every important meeting.

Develop and use ground rules to shape behavior and culture.

Publish meeting records promptly.

EXERCISE 1: ORGANIZATION STUDY

Fill out and submit the Initiative-to-Action form at the link in *Figure 73* for at least one of the initiatives you plan for your project organization to pursue:

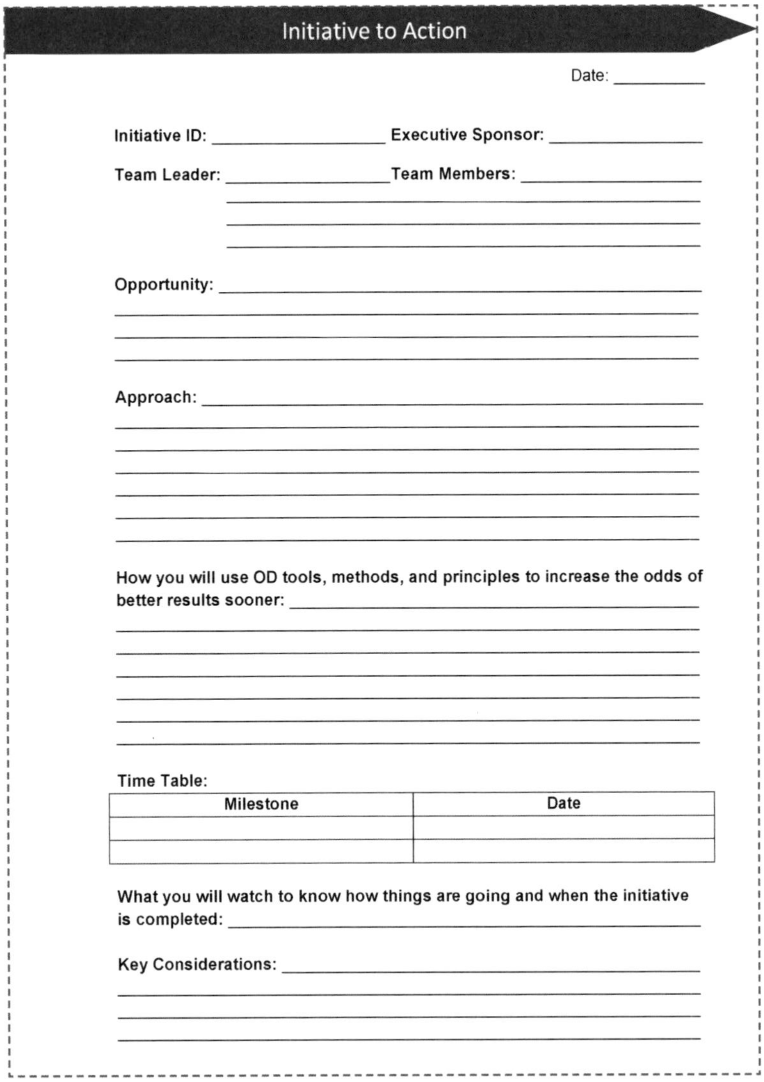

Initiative to Action

Date: _____

Initiative ID: _____   Executive Sponsor: _____

Team Leader: _____   Team Members: _____
_____
_____
_____

Opportunity: _____
_____
_____
_____

Approach: _____
_____
_____
_____
_____
_____
_____

How you will use OD tools, methods, and principles to increase the odds of better results sooner: _____
_____
_____
_____
_____
_____
_____

Time Table:

Milestone	Date

What you will watch to know how things are going and when the initiative is completed: _____

Key Considerations: _____
_____
_____
_____

Figure 73. *Link to Initiative-to-Action template. (http://www.intelliven. com/templates/initiative-to-action/)*

EXERCISE 2: ORGANIZATION STUDY

Fill out the cells in the exhibit below for at least one of the strategic initiatives you plan for your project organization to pursue:

Observed Behaviors	Inference	Target Behaviors	Interventions

Truth. No leader succeeds alone.

Action.

Get Help

Build a board. Retain experts.
Get a coach.

Get Help

Many CEOs and their leadership teams orchestrate meetings with their boards to:

- Show how great they are and how well things are going.

- Avoid leaving the meeting with more to do than when it started.

There is a lot more value that can be derived from working with the board but it takes a lot of work in building, cultivating, preparing for, and working with boards.

There are three distinctly different kinds of boards. People often mix up the three kinds of boards and things get very confusing. It is wise to be clear about what kind of board you are dealing with and to manage each accordingly.

A **Celebrity Board** is staffed with people who bring attention and prestige to the organization and who may provide access to potentially valuable resources (such as: money, clients, people to hire, or partners). Celebrity boards do not otherwise help organizations perform and grow much and so are not covered further here.

Advisory Board

A **Board of Advisors**, see *Figure 74,* is staffed with individuals with directly relevant personal experience in what the organization and its leaders are doing; e.g., they have first-hand experience in the industry dealing with the very same problems the organization faces and who provide valuable perspective and insight on best practices, benchmarks, and what will and will not work because they have been through it themselves.

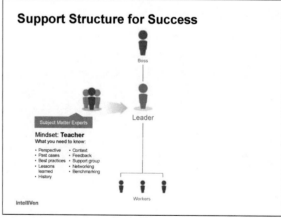

Figure 74. *Board of Advisors*

Advisory Board members generally have specific experience, knowledge, and perspective to draw on and that is often ideally tapped-into in a separate session with each outside advisor rather than as a group where each will struggle to find the way to deliver on why they think they have been recruited to participate in the first place while also jockeying for position and esteem from those present.

The **Sample Advisory Board Charter** in the Appendix shows how one organization's Advisory Board was set up. The organization's leaders routinely contact Advisory Board members to draw on their wisdom in key situations. The Advisory Board also meets as a group with a broad set of internal leaders two to four times a year for three or so hours at a

time. Background material on two or three of the most important things going on are prepared and sent to the members approximately two days ahead of the session along with specific questions that leadership wants help with. Members read the background ahead of time, think critically about what has been presented, and work hard to develop a point of view that they will share at the meeting. In the advisory meeting leaders talk through the key points, field clarifying questions from members, and then draw out their best advice for each of the items in turn.

Accountability Board

An **Accountability Board** (or Board of Directors or Governing Board), see *Figure 75* has a three-pronged charter (see Sample Board Charter (http://www.intelliven.com/wp-content/uploads/2012/02/Sample-Board-Charter.pdf)):

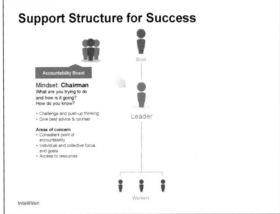

Figure 75. *Accountability Board*

- To provide a **consistent point of accountability** - where management puts before the board a plan and regularly reports on how things are going relative to plan.

- To help with **individual and collective focus** - what is it that the organization as a whole seeks to accomplish and how it is going, and what each of the C-level team members are specifically trying to accomplish and how is it going.

- To provide **access to resources** such as ideas, money, clients, people to hire, partners, and advisers.

- Accountability Board members may also attend and participate fully as Advisory Board members.

The Accountability Board meets four to six times a year for management to cover the following agenda:

- Here is what we said we would do.

- Here is what we actually did.

- Here is what happened.

- Here is what we learned.

- Here is what we plan to do next.

Materials are prepared, forwarded two or so days in advance (to give board members time to prepare and to allow the leadership team time to step back from the details of their material), and walked through in the meeting using the outline above much as for an Advisory Board meeting. Accountability Board members then ask questions to clarify and push-up management's thinking and then board members each offer their best advice.

Members of the leadership team who attend Accountability Board meetings must work hard to listen carefully to what members have to say through their questions and comments and without being the least bit defensive. The Board Chair works with the CEO to ensure that the environment is safe for management to say what needs to be said and to be sure that management hears what needs to be heard. To do so takes conscious cultivation and effort to intervene and give individual and group coaching when discussions go off track or when people talk past each other as often happens.

The organization's fiscal health is a key topic for every Accountability Board meeting. The organization's financial model, its financial plan, and its performance as reported in its income statement, cash flow, and balance sheet are constantly in focus and assessed carefully relative to past performance, planned performance, and performance relative to other organizations.

There are significant legal obligations that come with being a director of a legal corporation. For this reason, firms either buy their directors Director's & Officers Insurance (which is a significant expense) or call their governing board a Board of Advisors even though it functions as a Board of Directors but without the liability and also without the power to hire and fire the CEO.

WORK PROBLEMS: GET HELP

PROBLEM 1

Organization Dilemma:

A practice helps banks increase productivity in their credit operation. The number of people working has grown from 25 two years ago, to 50 last year, to 100 now. The leader can no longer keep up with everything and needs to delegate.

There appear to be three ways to carve-up responsibilities (see **Figure 76**):

- Put those responsible for customers in charge.

- Put those who supervise what people do (consult, design, develop, install, support) in charge.

- Put a person in charge of customers and what people do by region.

After reviewing the three options with staff, peers, bosses, family, and friends the leader has arranged a meeting with a prestigious organization development consultant to find out once and for all which course to follow.

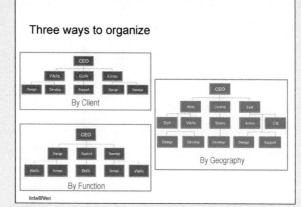

Figure 76. *An Organization Dilemma organization chart.*

To start their meeting the leader presents the background and a detailed organization chart for each option and talks through the pros and cons of each. After about 40-minutes she closes by saying she knows she is close to the answer but can't quite put her finger on it and just needs a little help to nail it. She ends by asking: **"Which of these is the right one and the one I should roll out?"**

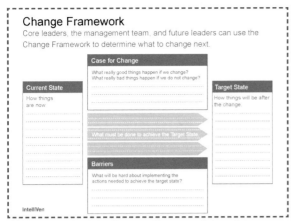

Figure 77. *Link to Change Framework template. (http://www.intelliven.com/templates/change-framework/)*

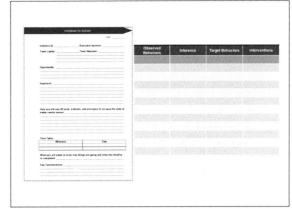

Figure 78. *Organization Dilemma Initiatives-to-Action Chart. (http://www.intelliven.com/templates/initiative-to-action/)*

How would you respond to the CEOs question if you were the outside consultant or a peer advisor?

- Review what the OD professional actually said:

PROBLEM 2

Click *Figure 77* to fill out and submit the change framework and the Initiative to Action form for the organization described in the work problem.

PROBLEM 3

Click *Figure 78* to fill out and submit the Initiative-to-Action template for the Organization Dilemma work problem.

What might a leader learn from this advice?

- There are things the leader didn't know

- There are ways for the leader to find out what she does not know

- It is ok not to know everything

- She can behave now in full knowledge and does not have to give credit to anyone for that knowledge

How might this input change the leader's life?

- Better at getting and seeking input

- Enlightened on an important element of organization dynamics, development, and evolution

- Increased instinct to seek help

- Now appears smarter and better informed to her team

- Looks and behaves more like a leader

- You never know when you are going to get gold (so always be open to it when it comes along)

What the OD consultant said:

There Is No One Right Organization	The organization that will work is the one a group decides to make work, after much study and debate, despite its flaws. It is easy to make any organization fail. It is harder to make one work. The group that bands together to design its own future and that then signs up to make it work every day is the one that is on track to success.
Organizations Change Slowly	It is often better to make small moves than to make wholesale changes. Organization change is hard on people. It helps to go slow, and to keep everyone clear about what is going on, why it is going on, and what is needed from them to succeed.
No Organization Is Forever	Each organization is a step along the way to the next. When an organization is put in place, it is a good time to also think about what might be next because it will not be long before adjustments are needed to stay on track to success. The best organizations develop a core competence at constant change.

intelliVen

Figure 79. *Organization change principles.*

Personal Effectiveness Coach

An OD consultant provides valuable input to the CEO and in a different way than does an Accountability Board or than do Subject Matter Experts. An OD Consultant, or Personal Effectiveness Coach, helps the leader understand and learn how to better work with people and to use him/herself in a thoughtful and intentional manner; see *Figure 80*[1].

Coaches can also be mentors, retired CEOs, experienced hands from personal or professional networks, family members who are willing and able to listen thoughtfully and say what needs to be said in a way it can be heard. The caution, though, is that input from untrained sources tends to be subjective and constrained by experience and competence of the source.

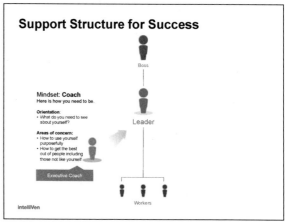

Figure 80. *Personal Effectiveness Coach*

---

1 Improving human interaction is a major focus of Organization Development and is well beyond the scope off Manage to Lead. Interested readers are encouraged to participate in a Human Interaction Lab or take a course of study in OD.

Peer Group

A group of Peers who run organizations of similar scope, scale, business type, industry served, and location run by a trained facilitator is an opportunity for leaders to be vulnerable and open to input. Peer groups (see *Figure 81*) are an excellent way to get perspective, learn by sharing and comparing, and to hold each other accountable.

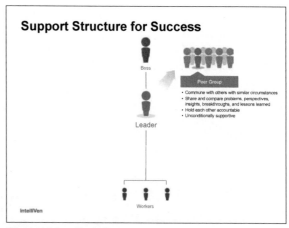

Figure 81. *Peer Group*

EXERCISE 1: ORGANIZATION STUDY

Click *Figure 82* to fill out and submit your organization's leadership support structure.

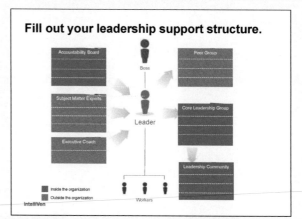

Figure 82. *Support Structure for Success template. (http://www.intelliven.com/templates/leadership-support-structure/).*

Summary

Arrange an operating framework of outside support from an accountability board, advisory board, and personal effectiveness coach.

- Keep Accountability Board separate from Advisory Board or subject matter experts.

- Build Accountability Board to provide help with accountability, focus, and resources.

- Work with a coach to get feedback on human interaction, facilitation, and team building.

- Commune regularly with a group of outside peers to get perspective, unconditional support, advice, and accountability.

Take input from untrained sources with caution.

Determine which of source of help to draw on based on the matter to address.

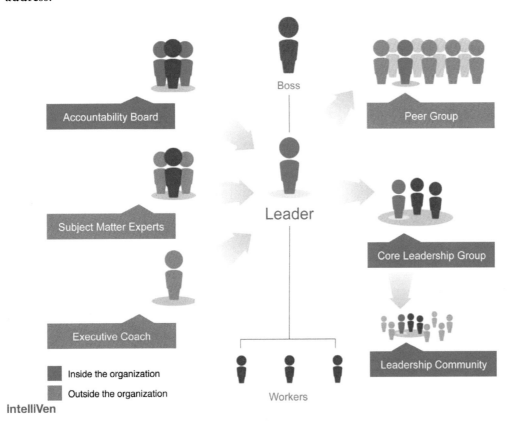

Truth. It's OK to do what you like and are good at.

Action.

Focus

Act intentionally, persist variously.

Focus

Leaders should consider the following when assigning tasks to leadership team members:

- Members of the leadership team are likely to be the most capable people in the organization and therefore among the most important to deploy optimally.

- Each needs to be especially clear about what is most important for him or her to do and then spend the majority of his/her time doing it.

- If something is important to do then someone important ought to be in charge of getting it done.

- Each member of the top team ought to be in charge of something important.

- It is not possible to be personally responsible for more than one or two important things at a time.

The idea is to ensure that at least what well-deployed team members focus on goes well and to model how things should be done for the rest of the organization. Leadership team members do not have to get everything right but they each have to **get something right**.

Penetrate Peaks

Most people, including even most senior executives, instinctively choose to spend their time doing many more than one or two things, as suggested by *Figure 83*: possibly because in their minds:

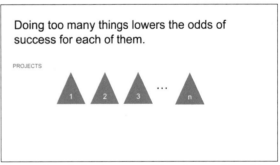

Figure 83. *Doing too many things lowers the odds of success for each.*

- Doing many things **increases the odds that something will go well.**

- Having **too many things to do** gives a great excuse for not being successful at any particular thing.

- The need to think hard about how to spend time is replaced by the easier decision to spend time based on urgent, but hardly ever important, demands that come from a never ending stream of urgent email, text, tweet, phone call, conversation, or knock on the door.

- Having many things vying for attention makes a leader feel powerful and busy, often to the point of having a "Hero complex".

On the other hand, having many things to do means that the most important people do not meet their goals because:

- Each task gets too little time, attention, and effort.

- Each leader works really hard but gets little done, gets tired, loses confidence, and feels ineffective yet has an inflated sense of self importance.

The leader's job is to make clear what is most important for each team member to do and to arrange for them to do it, and little-to-nothing else, even though it may cause team members to feel a greater risk of failure.

To solve the problem, the leader, as suggested in **Figure 84**, should:

- Work with each team member to rank their assignments in priority order.

- Ask if the odds of success on the most important task would go up if the team member were to spend more time on it. The answer will likely be, "Yes".

- Tell the team member to spend **all their time on the top priority** task until the odds of success would not get any better with any more time on it.

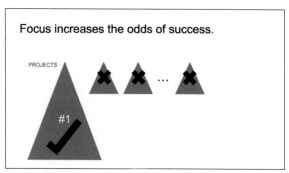

Figure 84. *Focus increases the odds of any success.*

Most team members will shudder at the thought of having so little to do when they realize it is now incumbent on them to be successful at just one important task. It occurs quickly that they might not be successful. When asked, "What if I fail?" the leader should express confidence that the team member will succeed and promise yet another important assignment in the event of failure.

The leader should add that if the team member puts everything into completing an assigned task but fails on six different assignments in a row, then maybe it will be time to discuss whether there is good fit with the organization. The point is to put the fear of failure far into the future in order to **free the team member to concentrate on what s/he has been asked to do** and not on the downside of failure. The downside risk moves from the team member to the leader who is then highly motivated to provide assistance, resources, governance, and incentives to maximize the odds of success.

Related Points:

- When a matter comes up for discussion, ask if it is important. If it is, then ask who is in charge of making sure it goes well. If no one comes to mind then assign someone or second guess its importance.

- When speaking with someone on the leadership team, ask what important thing they are responsible for completing. If nothing comes to mind then it is fair to wonder why they are on the leadership team.

- If something is not important then no one should even be thinking about it.

- Advise team members that while each may be able to manage many things it is generally possible to effectively lead just one or two.

Line up what a worker is good at and likes doing with what s/he wants to do.

In order to increase the odds of engagement, happiness, and high-performance leaders should learn what people on their team **like** to do and what they are **good at** doing so they can be aligned with what they **want** to be doing.

Many people want to do something different than what they like and what they are good at because they believe others think that something else is more valued as suggested by *Figure 85*. Great leaders tune into their team members to learn what each likes and is good at and then convinces them that what they **LIKE** and are **GOOD AT** is **VALUED** which causes them to **WANT** to do what they are good at and like doing and that the leader believes is important to do.

Alignment between Good at, Like, and Want achieved by the leader communicating what is Valued (as suggested by *Figure 86*) leads to improved engagement, and fulfillment across team members that individually and collectively have a much higher chance of achieving extraordinary results.[1]

Consider, for example, several who accomplished much (Steve Jobs, Daniel **Goleman, Krishna Dass, Ram Dass**) who all spent time in an Indian ashram with **Hindu guru Neem Karoli Baba** just as they were starting their careers. Guru Baba got to know them each well and used his status as their yogi to give them permission to be who they really are.

Most people have to figure out for themselves how to chart the course of a fulfilled life. The best leaders strive to play a role like that of the enlightened yogi and assign those in their organization to do what they are good at doing while also getting them to *want* to do what they are *good at*, and *like*, doing.

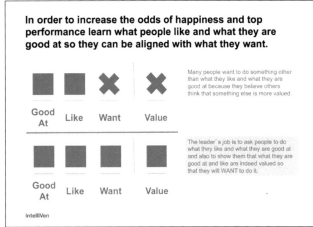

Figure 85.   *Good At, Like, Want, Value*

Figure 86.   *Align Good At, Like, Want, Value*

---

1 For more on achieving alignment for success see: Flow: The Psychology of Optimal Experience by Mihaly Csikszentmihaly; and The Doom Loop System by Dr. Dory Hollander; Steven Covey's Big Rock's Parable and his first three habits of highly effective people: end in mind, first things first, and be proactive; and Jim Collins's Hedgehog concept in *Good to Great.*

WORK PROBLEMS: FOCUS

EXERCISE 1

List your current assigned tasks including those that you should do but never get around to doing.

Arrange them in priority order.

Note how much time is spent on each over the course of a week.

Note how much time should be spent on each over the course off a week.

Note what would happen if you spent time the way you think you should.

What trade-offs would have to be made to spend time the way you should?

EXERCISE 2

List what you do for your organization.

Label for each thing that you do for your organization how much you like doing it and how good you are at doing it:

List what you most want to do for your organization.

List what your organization most wants you to do.

Note and comment on points of departure.

EXERCISE 3

List what you like doing.

List what you are good at doing.

List what you most want to do.

Explain the logic behind the alignment or lack of alignment between what you are good at doing, what you like doing, and what you want to be doing.

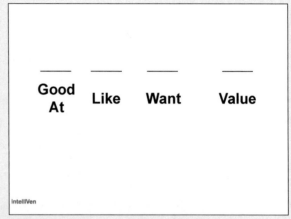

Figure 87. *Personal Alignment Chart*

List organizations that may need someone like you to do that which you like, are good at, and want to do.

Summary

Points related to focus apply both to leaders and to every team member.

To increase the odds of success **Penetrate Peaks** rather than **Propagating Pyramids**.

Play the role of yogi by getting leaders in your organization to do what you need them to do in a way that aligns with what they *want* to do and with what they are *good at*, and *like*, doing.

If there is nothing that a person does well and that s/he enjoys doing that is of great value to the organization then it may be time for that person to spend their time with another organization.

Make sure team members know that leaders value what they are good at and like doing so that they will want to do what they are good at and like doing.

Always know what is the one most important thing you are currently doing. If you do not know what the number one thing to do is then the number one thing to do is to figure out what is the most important thing that the organization is counting on you to do.

Spend the great majority of your time and effort on that one most important thing.

Ensure the same for every member of the team.

Truth. Growth is good.

Action.

Grow

Grow to increase value,
impact, and opportunity.

Grow

One could argue that everything covered to this point in *Manage to Lead* prepares the organization to grow. With a solid foundation laid, now is indeed time to grow.

Organization Evolution

Organizations almost always progress through five more-or-less well-defined evolutionary growth stages, as shown in the diagram in *Figure 88*:

- **Concept**
- **Start-up**
- **Credible**
- **Sustainable**
- **Mature**.

Each stage is defined by key characteristics, operating agenda, economics, and key concerns as summarized below.

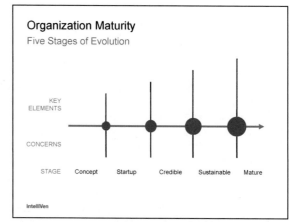

Figure 88.   *Five stages of organization evolution*

Concept Stage

A new organization starts out as an idea, or **Concept.** As suggested in *Figure 89* a bona fide **Concept** requires at least a rough outline of:

- What problem the organization is to solve for whom and how (http://www.intelliven.com/how-to-get-clear-about-what-problem-an-organization-solves-for-whom-how/).

- Some seed money to cover the cost of getting off the ground.

- A Core Leadership Team to bring the concept to reality.

It is hard to get a good idea, enough money, and a strong team all in the same place at the right time for success. Many search their entire careers for the right combination. Those who are successful once hardly ever are able to do it again. Despite the long odds, a million or so new for-profit, non-profit (https://www.6figurejobs.com/Career-News/Entrepreneur/Record-number-of-new-businesses-started-last-year-$100000909-438039519.html), and internal ventures are conceived each year in the U.S. (http://www.thenonprofittimes.com/news-articles/each-501c3-is-now/)

Whoever covers the costs of getting going generally owns the venture.

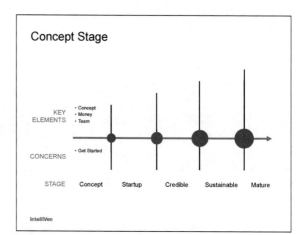

Figure 89.   *Concept stage*

Money to get out of the gate is often provided by the one who came up with the idea along with "family, friends, and fools (which some say are, by definition, all fools!)." People with money seek good ideas and strong teams in which to invest. Great teams search for ideas and money. Those with ideas search for money and strong players.

Those that launch a new venture are likely to have little, or no, leadership, management, or business experience. According to the Small Business Administration "two-thirds of new employer establishments survive two years, and 44 percent survive four years. (http://smallbiztrends.com/2005/07/business-failure-rates-highest-in. html)"[2] Nonetheless, founders with determination, energy, intelligence, wits, a sense of humor, and with a thirst to learn both from their mistakes and from others with experience, can do quite well.

Objectives in the **Concept** stage are to:

- Prepare a description of the organization that explains:
  - Whose problem it will solve and how it will solve it (page 20).
  - How the organization will find, sell, and serve customers (page 28).
  - How revenue, costs of generating revenue, cost of sales and support activities will generate, over time, financial stability and profit.

While there is nothing like learning through iterative trial and error, it is far more efficient (i.e., it costs less, takes less time, and is easier) to uncover and sort out challenges by thinking through and articulating a concept than through trial and error. It is also easier, and more likely to be unambiguous, to share a well-thought-out **Concept** with those who eventually join, invest in, or advise the organization.

- Clarify why it makes sense to bring the **Concept** to reality. For example:
  - **Wealth creation:** a venture may exist primarily to someday be sold, ideally at a price far greater than the cost of developing it, and the proceeds shared by those who helped make it happen. In this case, it helps to be clear from the start how much wealth meets the needs of those involved to increase the odds that everyone is on the same page and pulling for the same result.
  - **Income generation:** a venture may exist to provide a source of sufficient resources to it employs to finance their living. In this case, it helps to be clear about what level of income is sufficient to meet their needs.
  - **Impact:** a venture may contribute to the greater good; for example: create jobs, enhance lives, or otherwise improve the world in some specific way. In this case, it helps to know just what scope and scale of impact the founders have in mind.

---

2 See: https://www.6figurejobs.com/Career-News/Entrepreneur/Record-number-of-new-businesses-started-last-year-$100000909-438039519.html **and** http://www.thenonprofittimes.com/article/detail/each-501c3-is-now-2949

Clearly thinking through and articulating which of the above, including combinations, provides a guiding hand to what lies ahead.

- Find and study existing and past organizations that have been successful doing something similar to understand what they learned it takes to be successful. Contact those who were key to such organizations and run the **Concept** by them to get their input on lessons learned and to arrange for their on-going help.

- Organize a forum to serve as a **consistent point of accountability** for leaders to report on what they plan to do, what they actually do, what happened, what they learned, and what they plan to do next; get help with strategy and focus, and access to resources.

- Produce evidence that the **Concept** makes sense and that it can perform as imagined and therefore it is worth investing time and money to take to the next stage.

- Make as much progress with as little outside funding as possible. The more money taken-in, the more ownership is given away in the form of equity to investors. Giving up equity is disadvantageous to those responsible in that their ultimate financial return is less and significant amounts of time will be diverted to recruiting and managing investors at the cost of making progress on what their organization seeks to accomplish. When founders give up more than 50% of the ownership they are no longer in control and essentially become a project team reporting to outside owners who do not understand the business well enough to run it.

- Establish a leader and **leadership team** with relevant and complementary strengths and who get along well with each other. It is essential that it be clear who among the top team fills the role of leader. The leader and his/her team must have a common vision for what they seek to accomplish as well as the energy and drive to take action and make things happen. The team is often more important than their idea or the money because, after the first stage has played out, the team that wins is the team that learns from their experience to get it right next time. Until there is funding enough to pay salaries team members may continue to work elsewhere to finance their living.

Start-up Stage

The **Start-up**, see *Figure 90*, is when the product or service (WHAT) of the organization is created. Initially there may be has a few clients (WHO) and up to a few dozen employees who are gaining confidence that what they do fills a genuine need in a market (WHY)m where no other player dominates. On the other hand, survival is far from guaranteed.

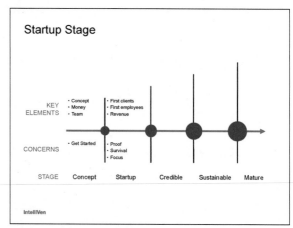

Figure 90. *Start up stage*

The **Start-up** is likely to be self-funded or a few investors may have kicked-in less than a million dollars, for a small equity stake. A fully-funded **Start-up** might have one serious institutional investor, with more waiting in the wings, who has invested $1-2M in return for up to 40% of the equity. The organization uses raised funds to cover the cost of developing its offerings and its sales, delivery, and operating methods.

The principal issues for **Start-up** organizations revolve around focus and managing scarce resources. For example, **Start-ups** often struggle to deploy scarce, competent personnel to both successfully deliver on commitments to current customers and to find the next customer. The few people who "know what they are doing" are spread precariously thin across sales and delivery activities and there never seems to be time or energy left at the end of each day to even think about anything long-term.

As hectic as it is to get through the day serving customers and prospects, there may simultaneously be a race-against-time to secure financial resources required to continue operating. Cash to a **Start-up** is like blood to a living being, or gas to a car, in that everything stops when it runs out so, until the organization starts making its own, there is an ever-present need to find more from the outside.

While the above is all-consuming enough, **Start-up** leaders often cannot resist temptation to allow their attention to wander in order to explore near-by or new opportunities believing that the "big-win" may be just around the corner. Launching such initiatives is tantamount to launching additional businesses.

A better strategy is usually to not "chase rainbows" and, instead, tighten focus further on the business that offers the best prospects for the most growth so that scarce resources can be optimally deployed to efficiently drive the most value. It is hard enough to run one business well and launching others reduces the odds of any success.[3]

Often a Start-up leader and team are challenged to decide to stick with and drive to scale a specific business model having become hooked on moving rapidly from one idea to the next. The risk is getting stuck in an infinite Start-up Phase and missing the opportunity to turn something small into something big.

Whether, and how, the organization evolves to systematically address these challenges will determine its attractiveness to current and future employees, customers and prospects, partners, suppliers, banks, investors, and suitors.

To stabilize operations sufficient to attract customers, employees, board members, financing, and partners, leaders develop a **strategic plan** and an operating plan that includes the elements listed below.

---

3 See also Jim Collins, Good to Great; Hedge Hog Concept.

STRATEGIC PLAN

- It's mission/purpose, vision, and values (http://www.skills2lead.com/)

- **What problem the organization solves for whom?** That is, what:

  - Market does the organization serve,

  - Problem that market has, and

  - Solution the organization provides the market to solve the problem.

- **How does the organization work?** That is, how does the organization find and convince decision-makers in the market to buy their solution and how does the organization develop, deliver, and service (i.e., do what the organization does) that solution? The principal systems of a business are its selling system and its doing system. The third system is the system it uses to grow. How does the organizations constantly develop and evolve their systems to:

  - Do,

  - Sell, and

  - Grow.

- **How well** does the organization do, sell, and grow compared to:

  - How others do it,

  - How the organization has performed in the past, and

  - How the organization said it would do?

  i.e., compared to industry benchmarks, historical benchmarks, and benchmark to plan

- **How does the organization know how well it is doing?** That is, what metrics does it watch and what processes are used to manage and control its do, sell, and grow systems?

- **What is most important to change next?** That is, how and why does the organization need to evolve from where it is now to some specific future, for what specific reasons, and in what specific way? How do the strategic initiatives change:

  - Systems;

  - Processes; and

  - Organization and in terms of how people are supposed to think and behave.

- A target financial model that shows revenue, direct costs, gross profit by revenue type, indirect labor and non-labor costs by function, operating profit, labor, headcount, and associated ratios for the prior year, by quarter for the current year and by year for one and two years into the future,

- Short-term initiatives and success criteria (e.g., land a new strategic customer generating significant revenue within so many months; operate with profit as a specific percent of net revenue; etc.),

- Key players, roles, responsibilities, goals, initiatives, and accountabilities associated with a pattern of achieving stated objectives,

- A systematic way to forecast and track:

  - financial performance against plan and

  - operating progress relative to strategic initiatives,

- Defined sales, delivery, governance, human resource, communications, and financial processes.

- A board of outside directors to provide consistent accountability, input on strategy and help with setting focus of the organization as a whole and for each of its operating leaders, and access to resources such as experience, best practices, training, money, and prospective employees, customers, investors, partners, and possible acquirers.

Leadership's mandate is to execute their strategy and operating plan while it tracks and reports on progress to establish a pattern of successful performance against plan. Stakeholders (owners, founders, management, board, employees) are anxious for the **Start-up** to achieve results that make it clear the organization is on a solid and predictable track to fulfill its mission and to generate returns on their financial and personal investments.

The organization's culture, or way of working, takes shape and hardens as does its core values or its beliefs that shape behavior.

Credible Stage

If a **Start-up**, see *Figure 91*, is about making pizza, a **Credible** organization is about a pizza-making business[4]. The agenda moves from getting things done to building systems that get things done. The odds of long-term growth and profitability increase the closer the organization holds to a proven way of working or business model, such as one of the following five:

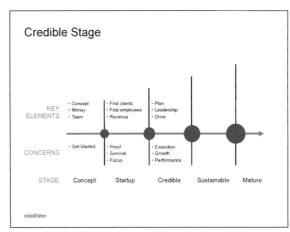

Figure 91. *Credible Stage*

- Service

- Product

- Operation

- Channel

- Exchange

and how well it executes its core delivery, sales, and capacity development in the face of increasing scale and complexity.

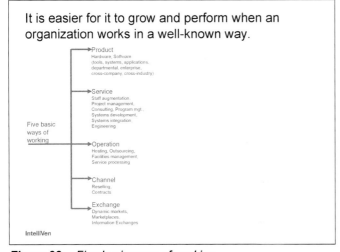

Figure 92. *Five basic ways of working.*

Kind of Operation	Output	Payment	Example
Product	Software, hardware, information. etc.	Per copy Per unit	Hewlett Packard Microsoft
Service	Hourly or project consulting or service	Per hour Per deliverable	Deloitte Booz Allen Hamilton
Operation	Outsourcing Facilities Management	Per unit of time Per unit processed	USInternetworking EDS outsourcing
Channel	Set up and administer connection between buyer and provider	Percentage of revenue	Amazon FedBid AOL
Exchange	Broker many buyers and many sellers	Subscription fee Transaction fee	NYSE, eBay

The way of working is defined largely by they way its financials work.

Figure 93. *Five ways of working defined*

---

4 See Michael Gerber, e-Myth Revisited, ibid.

More specifically, an organization's way of working (or business model) determines:

- The way its **finances** work

- Its **sales** and **delivery** processes

- The **competencies** it needs to develop

- Its **competitive landscape**

- Its target valuation as a function of prospects for **operating income as a percent of revenue** and **growth**

- Exit alternatives, potential buyers, and timing

- Expansion prospects and targets

- The degree of **risk** and **difficulty**

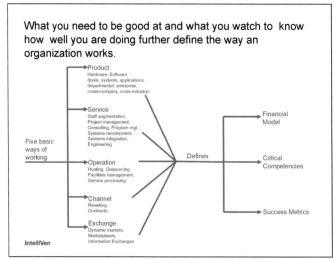

Figure 94. *Each way of working has its own financial model, critical competencies, and performance metrics.*

It is harder to perform and grow reliably with multiple or hybrid ways of working.

Way of Working	Financials	Competencies	Metrics
Product	EBIT=20% P/E=100X	Sales, Call Center, Development	# of salesmen, salesmen tenure, $/sale, $/salesman
Service	EBIT=15% P/E=25X	Project Management Account Management	Staff utilization Average hourly rate
Operation	EBIT=10% P/E=10⁺X	Efficiency of operation Driving to scale	Cost per unit Service levels
Channel	EBIT=3% P/E=5X	Contract management & administration Space, Inventory Mgt	Contract order backlog Commitment level
Exchange	EBIT<0 P/E=n.a.	Domain competence Efficiency of operation	Number subscribers Number of transactions

IntelliVen

Figure 95. *Five ways of working and associated financials, competencies, and performance metrics.*

See how one W-W-W can be supported by any of many approaches.

Which way of working is right for Castro Crane?

Castro Crane:
Locates, fixes, and resells secondhand cranes throughout the world

IntelliVen

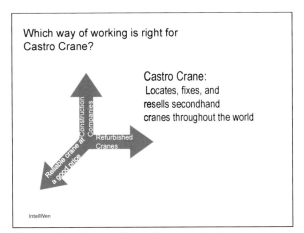

Figure 96. *Castro Crane Market - Problem - Solution*

Castro Worksheet

For any given solution, there are often many ways to deliver it.

Customer: Construction Companies; Problem: Reliable Cranes; Solution: Refurbished Cranes	
Product	Build, or procure and refurbish, cranes to sell
Service	Assess, recommend, and service cranes
Operation	Own, maintain, and operate cranes for rent
Channel	Connect crane buyers and sellers
Exchange	Broker link between crane seekers and crane owners who bid to sell their cranes

IntelliVen

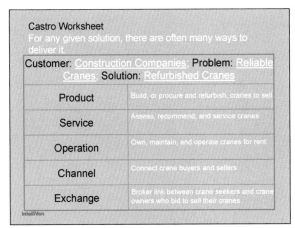

Figure 97. *Castro Crane Worksheet*

Choose which business model is best based on key factors.

- What organization leaders are good at doing and what they like to do.
- Resources available (e.g., people, money, time).
- Economic returns sought.
- Appetite for risk.

IntelliVen

Figure 98. *How to choose the way to work.*

A new way of banking with the Internet.

Customer: Banks; Problem: Customer Access; Solution: Phone, Branch, Mail + Internet	
Product	Sell software to enable access via Internet (S1)
Service	Hourly services to help banks develop own Internet front-end (AMS)
Operation	Operate a service by the account/month to let bank customers access via Internet (ORCC)
Channel	Connect banks to suppliers of Internet front-end software (Accenture)
Exchange	Match any of several banks with any of several front-ends based on needs, price, and availability (e-Loan)

IntelliVen

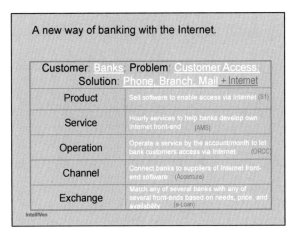

Figure 99. *A new way of banking with the Internet*

It is critical to determine the key source of revenue around which to build the business. While it may be possible to build around multiple revenue sources, it is a hard enough to do around just one revenue source. It is, therefore, best to pursue multiple sources only after at least one is on a solid track for success.

Organizations in the **Credible Stage** are characterized by a consistent and growing base of revenue and profit, a **financial plan,** an **operating plan,** and **core leaders in place** who are clear about what the organization is counting on from each of them, and a **track record** of consistently achieving planned performance. Core leaders are responsible for developing and delivering on their plan and driven to achieve or exceed planned levels of performance by an incentive program that rewards success for so doing.

Sustainable Stage

If a business does a few things right in its early stages of evolution, it can markedly improve the odds of sustaining accelerated growth and outstanding performance. Conversely, it is very difficult for an organization to make critical adjustments to its operating characteristics once it has achieved scale and maturity. Designing the organization well in the **Startup Stage** improves attractiveness to all its stakeholders.

Sustainable Stage organizations are characterized by increasing the share of market they target and putting competitors out of the picture either through acquisition or outperforming them. A key concern of organizations that make it to the **Sustainable Stage** is to create liquidity for those who have helped get it there.

Mature Stage

Key concerns of a mature venture are:

- Continuing to perform well against plan.
- Investing to find the next new thing that will drive growth.
- Positioning for an exit.
- Holding the attention and interest of key leaders (consider, for example, what happened in terms of new ideas and drive once the Core Leadership Group at Microsoft had become wealthy enough to each own an island or two).
- Finding new sources of growth in the face of approaching market saturation which may lead to spawning initiatives that then each progress through the five stages of organization evolution.

The following two tables illustrate how top leaders change as the organization evolves:

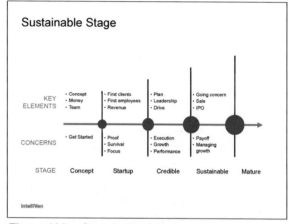

Figure 100. *Sustainable Stage*

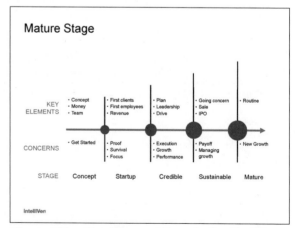

Figure 101. *Five Stages of Organization Evolution*

TABLE 1: THE ROLE OF THE CEO AND EXECUTIVE TEAM
CHANGES BY STAGE OF ORGANISATION MATURITY.

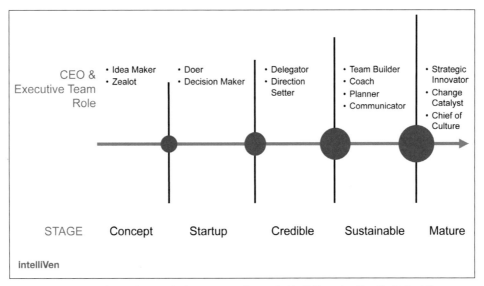

Adapted from Catlin & Cookman Group's Building the Profit Spiral ®

TABLE 2: LEADERSHIP TRAITS BY STAGE OF MATURITY
CHARACTERISTICS OF EVOLVING LEADERS

ROOKIE LEADER	KEY BEHAVIOR CHARACTERISTIC	HIGH-END LEADER
As a chore to get through	Views Administrative Processes ⟷ (E.g., Goal setting, Project reviews, Planning)	As a way to build the practice/business
Loose collection of projects	Unique selling proposition ⟷	Clearly defined market, problem, & solution and a plan to drive to scale
Capability based	Offering ⟷	Efficiently solves a high-order, high-stakes, important and pervasive business problem in a repeatable way
Knows what conferences leaders attend	Market Stature ⟷	Recognized leader in the industry
"My way or the highway"	Corporate Culture ⟷	Models and helps define and cultivate the way we want things to be
None; goes so far as to hide available resources for selfish reasons	Time spent for the corporate good ⟷	Significant but not so much as to distract from the primary mission to build the unit
Every project, sale, and hire is a whole new adventure	Respect for process ⟷	Mature execution, sales, and capacity development methodology
Antagonistic or defensive in dealings with other strong executives	Engages other Executives ⟷	Constructively adds insights, challenges prevailing opinions, and pushes to greater understanding through discourse; works the point not the person; seeks first to understand

TABLE 2: CONTINUED

ROOKIE LEADER	KEY BEHAVIOR CHARACTERISTIC	HIGH-END LEADER
Insecure, threatened by other strong players	Synergizes	Secure; able to construct and use interdependent relationships with other strong players; seeks win-win
Shuns feedback and input	Seeks Feedback	Aggressively seeks input and feedback on personal performance, ideas, and behavior
Enervates colleagues, subordinates, and superiors	Energizes Colleagues	Energizes colleagues, subordinates, and superiors
Tends to provide only positive feedback to avoid having to deal with giving more thoughtful, constructive and useful feedback	Provides Feedback	Provides thoughtful, constructive, and useful feedback and input to colleagues, subordinates and others who ask for it in order to help them grow.
Reactive—decides what to do on any given day based on what comes in on email, phone messages, knocks on door	Initiative to Drive the Business	Proactive; develops, holds, communicates, and drives to achieve a specific vision for the future business Sets aside large blocks of time to spend each day on what is most important (penetrate pyramid vs. propagate peaks) (big rocks)
Sends and receives communication when necessary (even urgent) to do so	Communication	Sets up, stimulates, and actively uses both input and outgoing channels (asks, lunches, All Hands, Updates, Weekly email, blog, tweets, reviews, etc.)
Look at where things ended up in hind-sight and explain after the fact…well after it is too late to do anything about it	Metrics	List of key performance metrics and target measures based on stage of evolution and industry norms for like organizations of similar evolutionary stage Follows a disciplined plan-project-do-review model to always know where things are going to be, why, and doing something about it using the what, why, so what, now what framework
Dog-and-pony show; defends against inquiries; work hard to make it look like everything is covered, all is well, and we don't need any more help or anything more to do thank you very much	Accountability Board	Systematically convenes outside reviewers with great and diverse strengths to review what you said you would do, what you did, what happened, what was learned, and what you plan to do next followed by non-defensive Q&A to push up thinking and then collect best advice from each member
Expects senior personnel to do the job they are well paid to do and to let the boss know how things are going from time to time and to get in touch when help is needed	Governance	Conducts weekly 1x1 sessions with each direct report to review top priorities, progress from prior session items, performance metrics, and any impediments to progress Regular executive committee meetings with topmost core team of leaders with complementary strengths and compatible orientations all out to accomplish the same thing with intent to give credit for any and all success to everyone else. Keeps and builds agenda between meetings, sent out in advance, with record of key insights, decisions, and action items prepared immediately following and used to drive activity between meetings and to set up for next meeting

TABLE 2: CONTINUED

ROOKIE LEADER	KEY BEHAVIOR CHARACTERISTIC	HIGH-END LEADER
Everyone helps the leader to be successful	Roles, Goals, and Rewards ⟵⟶	Leader helps everyone else be successful. Clear about what is wanted from every member of the team and has communicated that desire to the team member, wants the team member to do so, and believes the team member will be successful in so doing while also verifying that the team member understands their responsibility, wants to do it, and believes they can be successful doing it…and knows what to watch in order to monitor progress along the way. Ensures that team members have the resources (time, money, knowledge, training, books, advisors, etc.) needed to be successful in their assigned role Ensures that team members will be properly and fully rewarded in terms of cash, equity, praise, title, recognition, etc. individually and collectively for successfully accomplishing their goals
Don't need reviews as updates on status are covered in conversation on the fly or as necessary; meetings to discuss status, progress, and problems are rarely held and when they are held, they are held captive by the eight reasons reviews underperform	Reviews ⟵⟶	Used to: systematically keep top-of-the-house connected to the front-line showcase up-and-coming talent heighten stakes for team leaders to motivate top performance cross-fertilize lessons learned (in both directions) ensure the best possible knowledge, practices, ideas and resources are brought to bear in every instance institutionalize lessons learned Preparation allows manager and top team to: Work on what they are doing not just "in" what they are doing Presents what they seek to accomplish, what they have done to do so, what happened, and what they learned and what they plan to do next followed by inviting questions that are fielded non defensively and finally solicit and receive best advice. Action items, insights, and decisions are recorded and distributed for use between reviews and examined for follow up prior to the next review.
Meetings tend to be group gropes or forums for most senior member to feel important or powerful	Meetings ⟵⟶	Uses meetings in a topical area (project, program, functional area, key initiative, governance forum, sales opportunity, etc.) as a foil to drive progress in advance of the meeting and to purposefully architect meetings in terms of their Purpose, Objectives, Approach, and Deliverables using the How to Make Meetings Work framework during the meeting and uses the period following meetings to follow through on items from session while simultaneously beginning to prepare for the next meeting
Leads through application of their own sheer ability, energy, and drive	Core Team ⟵⟶	Builds a team of 3-7 players each with their own extraordinary strengths who are driven to accomplish a common result, love spending time together, and give all the credit for any success to others.
Seeks to ensure that he/she always looks good	Ego ⟵⟶	In-check; Works the point not the person

TABLE 2: CONTINUED

ROOKIE LEADER	KEY BEHAVIOR CHARACTERISTIC	HIGH-END LEADER
Always needs to be right	Vulnerability ←——————→ (a la Lencione)	Ok being wrong in front of the group
Thinks new leaders should be able to jump in and come up swimming as the top guy did in his day and especially how much it costs to find the person and to pay him or her	New Leader Transition ←——————→	Realizes that introducing a new leader initially takes more (not less) time and needs to be a thoughtful, purposeful exercise guided and led by the top executive to whom the new leader reports (see note on New Leader Transition Assistance).
Thinks they are supposed to know everything and that it is a weakness to seek or take input from others	Outside input ←——————→	Actively seeks out, engages, and draws on outside resources to provide subject matter (technical, process, industry) advice and personal effectiveness council.
Do what I say to do because I say so.	Guidance and direction ←——————→	Do what I say because you believe it is right to do and you want to do it. Get those who do not understand why and who do not want to do it to ask about it.
		Ask people to do what they Like and what they are Good at so that they will Want to do it.
Wings it	Preparation ←——————→	Prepares, shows up, Pays attention, develops a Point of view, Participates, does not dominate.
Does not draw an organization chart as it might put off some people.	Organization ←——————→	Develop and communicate a chart depicting the organization of responsibilities.
Does not make organizational realignments because it is too much trouble to get people to go along with it		No one right organization exists. The one that works is the one that everyone agrees to do all they can to make it work despite is flaws.
Make frequent major reorganizations		No organization is forever. Every organization is just a step along the way to the next. Organizations change best when they change slowly.
Listens but doesn't hear input from others thinking that all ideas have to come from the boss	Input ←——————→	Graciously and assertively takes input from subordinates, peers, bosses and advisors to consolidate, communicate, nurture, and drive to achieve a point of view reflecting input from all stakeholders.
Trades in all aspects of life for one dimensional quest…usually work-related.	Balance ←——————→	Sees professional pursuits as but one dimension in a balanced life.

EXERCISE 1: ORGANIZATION STUDY

Prepare for and hold an Executive Session for your organization as if you are its CEO. Hold the meeting with reviewers who are experienced CEOs, board members, or consultants to CEOs using the following POAD:

PURPOSE

Introduce a Student in the role of CEO to:

- The rigors of consolidating what they are doing in order to share with an accountability board
- The value of peer-review in a constructive and developmental forum
- A clear path to a higher probability of a better result, sooner

OUTCOMES

Hard Outcomes:

- Management presentation of what the Student CEO's organization is trying to do and how it is going
- Insights, ideas, and action items from having prepared and presented to a highly qualified and interested outside advisors and peer
- Ideas as to what else can be done to provide immediate and sustained value to the Student CEO's business

Soft Outcomes:

- Student CEO
    - Feels good about themselves, the work they did to prepare, and the value derived from presenting their material to others
    - Sees value from preparing for and working with this forum
- Reviewers
    - Have a good sense for the Student CEO and their strengths, developmental potential, approach, weaknesses, uptake capacity, disposition, and their openness to input and to being vulnerable
    - Enthusiasm for getting to know and to work further with the Student CEO and their top team were the opportunity to do so present

Approach

To prepare for your executive session, pull together a few slides to address to the following from your organization's CEO perspective:

- Current state (i.e. how things are now)
- Case for change (i.e. why things need to change)
- Target state (i.e. how things will be when they are the way they should be after they are changed.)
- What needs to be done in order to move the organization from the current state to the future state (i.e. strategic initiatives), and
- What will be hard about going from present to future state
- Arrange to have one or two executives senior to you serve as reviewers.

Use the Change Framework with one page of bullets for each of the five segments.

Deliverables

• Polish executive briefing.

• Work with a classmate or colleague to dry-run.

• Send to your reviewer.

Conduct executive session. Fill out meeting record and send to reviewers with expressed appreciation for their assistance. Revise your presentation materials to reflect input from the reviewer.

EXERCISE 2: ORGANIZATION STUDY

Note what the leader of your organization is doing to drive intentional change.

• Of the things we covered so far, what is the CEO doing?

• What is the CEO doing that has not been covered?

• What of the things covered is the CEO doing that s/he could/should be doing?

Dashboards

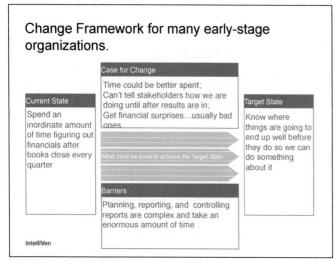

Figure 102. *Change framework for many early-stage organizations.*

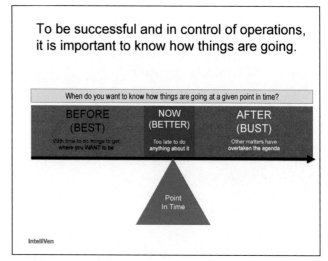

Figure 103. *To be successful and in control of operations, it is important to know how things are going.*

To be in control of operations always know at any given point in time:

• Where you want to go.

• Where you have been.

• Where you are headed next.

• Where you expected to be.

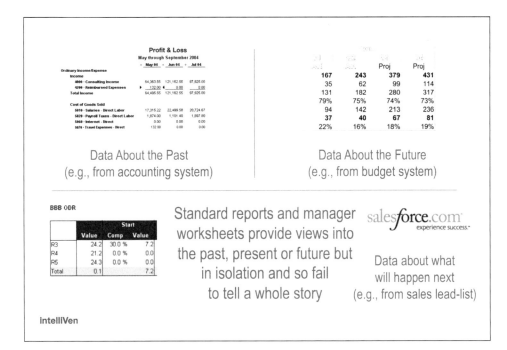

Figure 104. *Conventional reports help but do not show the flow from past to the present and into the future in order to construct and tell the full story about how an organization is performing.*

A Dashboard Provides:

• A high-level presentation of actual, projected, and planned key performance measures as compared to target, plan, and projected performance over a rolling, fixed period of time.

• Provides a path to detailed performance data, by type and reporting unit, that aggregates to the dashboard summary.

• Explains why results are different than projected and why projected are different than plan.

• Used to develop and tell a story about operations that makes sense and that top executives believe is correct and that they can compel others to believe in.

Four steps put leaders in control of operations using Dashboards.

Step-I: For finances, cash, resources, and labor:

• Identify key performance measures as in the left column of **Figure 105**.

• Set target values for each measure based on industry benchmarks as in the right column of **Figure 105**.

• Develop a plan to achieve them over time as in **Figures 106 and 107**.

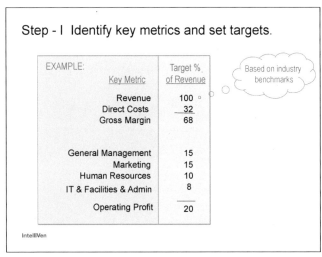

Figure 105. *Identify target metrics for chosen measures.*

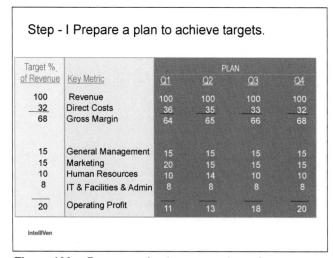

Step - I Prepare a plan to achieve targets.

Target % of Revenue	Key Metric	PLAN			
		Q1	Q2	Q3	Q4
100	Revenue	100	100	100	100
32	Direct Costs	36	35	33	32
68	Gross Margin	64	65	66	68
15	General Management	15	15	15	15
15	Marketing	20	15	15	15
10	Human Resources	10	14	10	10
8	IT & Facilities & Admin	8	8	8	8
20	Operating Profit	11	13	18	20

IntelliVen

Figure 106. *Prepare a plan to progress towards targeted results.*

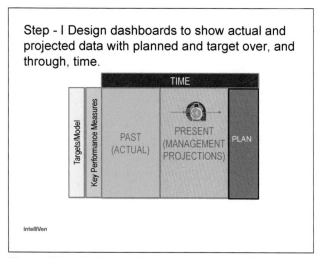

Step - I Design dashboards to show actual and projected data with planned and target over, and through, time.

IntelliVen

Figure 107. *Design dashboards to show actual and projected data with planned and target over, and through, time.*

Step-II: Design, implement, and drive Do & Review processes to:

- Set goals, project performance, perform, collect and compare actual results with projected.

- Explain variances, learn from the experience, adjust as appropriate, and re-project until goal achieved.

Step-III: Build a dashboard (see ***Figure 108***) to track progress using:

- Actual data about past performance.

- Management projections about the present and near-term performance.

- Planned future performance.

Step-IV: Identify selling, delivery, and scaling improvements to progress toward target; upgrade; drive to scale.

Step - III There are two basic ways to build dashboards.

IntelliVen

Figure 108. *Two ways to build dashboards*

WORK PROBLEMS: GROW

PROBLEM 1: DISGRUNTLED CLIENT

The Executive Vice President of one of your organization's top three clients has asked to speak with your CEO immediately. It is clear that your client is seriously disgruntled because of their perceptions of work performed by people in your organization.

- Who do you have handle this?

- What should s/he do?

- How should s/he prepare?

- What should be done afterwards?

When you have a disgruntled client, there are three things to do in order to get things back on track:

Unload the negative - In a face-to-face meeting, first invite your client to inform you of all the things that are bothering him/her in great detail. Ask clarifying questions to draw out and completely understand exactly what the trouble is. It is very important to repeat back each point in order to get explicit confirmation that you understand exactly what has been said. It is equally important to avoid contradicting the client, imposing your views, or defending against what is being said in any way. This task is complete when the client has said everything that is on his/her mind and when you have recapitulated with a complete summary of all of the points that have been brought to your attention. While you may be itching to tell your side of the story and to correct any misinformation, stay calm, repress such urges, and stick with the guidance above. It takes great self-control to do, but just keep asking for more, and recapitulate again, until the client has no more to say and they are completely sure you have heard them accurately. The point here is that it will be a great deal easier for your client to hear and listen to you after they have been heard.

Transition to positive - In the same meeting, next establish a basis of trust and credibility with a forthright, honest and sincere apology for anything you have done wrong and a firm statement about your interest and intent to do what it will take to make things right. Every sword still in its sheath must be laid on the table so that there are no barriers between parties which would inhibit moving forward. Ask the client if they would like to hear your perspective on the same points just raised. If so, share your version of the facts. The objective is to create an atmosphere of mutual interest and understanding that leads naturally to a joint desire to move forward. If the client is not interested in your side of the story or if they refuse to imagine that there is anything you could do to get on track for success, then there is not much point in going further.

Take positive action - The third step in the same meeting is to make a concession so that your client feels they are getting something to make amends even if you still believe their claims have no merit. Then lay out and initiate actions that prove you are committed to moving forward and to make things right. Positive action, no matter how small, is absolutely vital to close out the meeting. The number one reason things go wrong is lack of management attention. Assure your client that you will stay involved in order to make sure things stay on track and their needs will be met. Then follow through by paying attention, staying in touch, and making sure things come out right.

Each of these three steps must be taken and worked through to completion in one session and in the order presented. To prepare for the session, compile the facts as you understand them so that in step one you can be listening to discover what they client knows or has experienced that you may not know and so that in the second step you have an organized, orderly and unemotional presentation of what you have to say. Be creative in step three. Find a way to give something in order to get something so that both parties feel that they have come out ahead and to lay the groundwork for a long and fruitful relationship.

WORK PROBLEMS: GROW, CONTINUED

PROBLEM 2: PERFORMANCE APPRAISAL SYSTEM

In groups of three or four, discuss the following and what you would do in the case described below:

The CFO, CTO, and COO and each of their four direct reports in a fast-growing, high-performing organization are doing well individually and collectively. Up to now these folks have not had a formal annual performance assessment. Each has great strengths, contributes mightily to helping the organization meet its annual goals. Each also has room for growth and development though they are also nearly blind to their own opportunity along these lines. The CEO desires to implement a high-impact performance appraisal process that doesn't take forever to complete and that lets each key employee know how much the organization values them and their contributions and that makes crystal clear what each should work on improving next.

This answer is written up as a blog post (http://www.intelliven.com/how-to-provide-employees-with-powerful-feedback-and-guidance-while-also-showing-that-the-organization-knows-and-appreciates-who-they-are-and-what-they-do/):

PROBLEM 3: WHAT'S WRONG WITH THE NUMBERS?

You stare in disbelief at the Q3 earnings report just handed to you by your trusty CFO (see below):

EQ3 Earnings Report

Revenue	Projected	Actual	Delta	%Delta
	($000)			
Services	1,325	1,342	17	1%
License	2,837	2,406	(431)	-15%
Maintenance	683	682	(1)	0%
Total Revenue	4,845	4,430	(415)	-9%
Gross Margin	3,841	3,418	(423)	-11%
Indirect Costs	2,538	2,500	(38)	-1%
Net	1,303	918	(385)	-30%
Margin	26.9%	20.7%	(0.06)	-23%

Q3 License Fees

License Fee Revenue	Actual ($000)
FEMA	500
EPA	750
DoT	275
DC Housing	881
Total License Fees	2,406

License Revenue Tracker ($000)

	Prospect	% Probability	License	Weighted
Highly Probable	Federal Emergency Relief Program	95%	500	475
	Environmental Protection Agency Experimental Roadways	95%	750	713
	Department of Transportation Volpe Center (Boston)	95%	275	261
	Total Highly Probable		1,525	1,449
Targeted	DC Housing	75%	881	661
	Transcom	75%	970	728
	Total Targeted		1,851	1,388
	Total Close-in Pipeline		3,376	2,837

WORK PROBLEMS: GROW, CONTINUED

How could actual results be 30% less than the projection you turned in just 13 days earlier? You notice right away that services and maintenance revenue and indirect costs are all just about on projection but license fees are off by 15%. You look at the License Revenue Tracker that backed-up your projection for license revenue that came from the VP of sales as you try to keep from seething:

How could the license revenue projection have been so wrong? You reach for the phone to ring your VP of Sales when it hits you:

- What happened?

- Why did it happen?

- What is learned because of what happened?

- What should you and the Sales VP do differently from now on when preparing license projections?

- A Revenue Forecast asserts that a certain amount of revenue will be earned in a certain period of time with a certain probability that the actual result will be within a certain tolerance of the forecasted result. For example: management may forecast there is a 90% chance of actual revenue being more than 10% less than a certain amount.

- % probability of revenue from a source is assigned by management based on their judgment in the face of their collective past experience with similar situations and similar circumstances.

- Some managers set their forecasts to equal the Expected Value (Sum of entries each multiplied by their assigned probability of occurring). There are potential problems with this approach in that:

   1. It allows fractional results, For example, $100,000 with a 50% probability of occurring would contribute $50,000 to the forecast even though the actual result will either be $0 or $100,000. Actual Results are more likely to binary because the sale either happens or it doesn't so fractional results do not occur.

   2. % probabilities assigned often reflect the probability of the revenue ever occurring but do not capture the period in which the revenue will occur. A good approach to forecasting needs to set the probability of revenue in a specific period.

   3. % probabilities assigned often reflect stage of progression through to a sale but do not represent a real assessment of probability. For example, one might assign a 75% probability to all prospects for which a proposal has been submitted because at this point they are 75% of the way through the sale process but it may be, in reality, that only 50% of all proposals are successful.

The way for management to prepare a forecast is to think carefully and critically about each possible sale in order to reach an informed judgment as to whether the projected revenue will happen in the period or that it won't and then, in the face of that thinking, compute a projection that has the target % chance (where target is probability around 90%) of being no worse than a degree of tolerance (say 10%) below the forecast. This takes careful, critical and rigorous thinking than most people are willing to invest but when they do, it pays off and they get better at it over time.

PROBLEM 4: GROWTH THROUGH ACQUISITION PART A

Your organization has decided to grow through acquisition. The long-time, venerable CFO has no experience with scaling through significant organic growth or through acquisition. He saw the handwriting on the wall and so has chosen to announce his retirement due to stress illness and desire to spend time with ailing parents and spouse. A process that leads to finding a stellar replacement is mandatory.

What do you do?

- Convene top team.

- Agree on competencies required and cultural behaviors sought. Consider technical skill requirements in Accounting & Finance, Cash Management, and Mergers & Acquisitions, as well as cultural fit. Decide how to

Effectiveness vs. Systems and Process Maturity

One way to think about an organization is in terms of both how good it is at doing what it does, that is its effectiveness, and how mature are its systems and processes for doing what it does. *Figure 109* shows a way to map organizations into a framework that uses both dimensions.

As shown in *Figure 110* organizations in the upper-right quadrant are good at what they do and are highly developed in terms of their systems and process maturity. Organizations such as Apple, Accenture, and IBM come to mind as known both for being very good at what they do and for having well-developed systems and processes that guide how they work.

In the lower right are organizations that have mature systems and processes but that are not known for being particularly good at what they do. Some government agencies, utilities, and highly bureaucratic organizations come to mind.

The lower-left-quadrant is where most people put the dotcoms (or "dot-bombs") of the late '90s. To work in lower-left-quadrant organizations might feel like being in a squirrel cage where there is always a lot of activity but there may not be much getting accomplished.

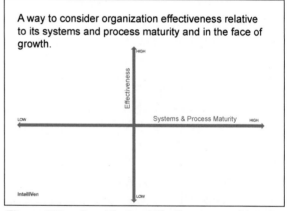

Figure 109. *Organization Effectiveness vs. Maturity*

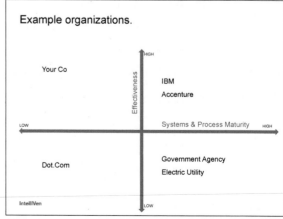

Figure 110. *Example organizations.*

Many early-stage organizations see themselves in the upper-left quadrant believing they are very good at what they do and proud to have little-to-no systems and processes that constrain them in any way. Everything that needs to happen just happens and everyone pitches in to get things done. The freedom from bureaucracy is exhilarating; especially for those who have previously worked in places that had a lot of rules and systems whether they were good at what they did or not.

Organizations that enjoy being in the upper-left quadrant sometimes find that, as they grow in terms of size (also called: scale) and/or complexity, effectiveness degrades as shown in *Figure 111*. Key players get overloaded with too many important things to do and it is no longer possible to keep everyone abreast of everything. Mistakes and suboptimal decisions are more common and it takes longer to get things done.

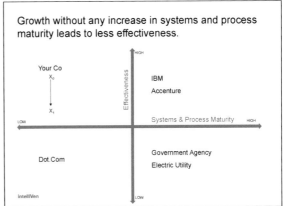

Figure 111. *Effectiveness can drop in the face of growth with no new systems and processes.*

Leaders in an upper-left organization whose effectiveness has started to slip may realize they need to implement systems and processes and so bring in an executive from an upper-right to bring order-to-chaos and to prepare for even more growth. While it may seem to be a reasonable strategy to bring in an experienced executive from an upper-right organization those doing so should be aware that it seldom goes well. The reason is that those from right-side organizations are so used to having access to well-developed resources, systems, and processes that they will be totally ineffective working in an organization that does not have them.

They are so used to having troops to deploy to get things done, for example, that when they want to get things done when in the upper-left, they fail to recognize that there are no troops. That is, they themselves are now the troops; an uncomfortable position to be in to say the least.

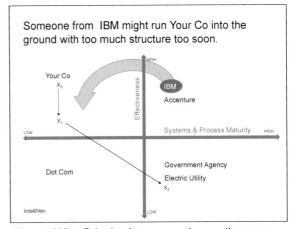

Figure 112. *Bringing in seasoned executives can bury emerging organizations.*

Even worse, as suggested by *Figure 112*, their instinct may be to recreate the order and maturity left behind whether it makes sense to do so or not. The scenario leads to drowning the up-and-coming organization in unnecessary bureaucracy given its stage of evolution. Because of this, many say that IBM executives do well in their second job after leaving because it takes one to learn that not everywhere works like IBM and not everywhere needs to work like IBM to be successful.

A preferred strategy is to add only those systems and processes required to maintain or even to improve effectiveness as suggested in *Figure 113*. As increases in growth and complexity require, the cycle repeats and the organization gradually migrates to the upper

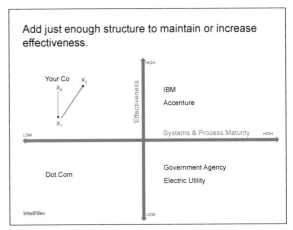

Figure 113. *Add just enough systems and processes to maintain or improve effectiveness.*

right. The evolution takes a long time but it works more smoothly and makes more sense. The process is much like a tennis or golf professional who works with emerging athletes on the one aspect of their game to provide the most lift next instead of trying to fix everything all at the same time.

Organizations that grow in terms of scale and complexity should expect to have to add systems and processes to get leverage, maintain order, and to lay the foundation for even more growth as they maintain and even improve their effectiveness (as summarized in *Figure 114*). It is also a good idea to add experienced executives to their top team but also wise to be sure those they do add have proven that they can operate effectively in an early-stage venture and that they are able to discern that which makes the most sense to do next as opposed to racing too fast to the upper-right.

As the organization performs and grows, its leaders find they need to spend more and more time working **On** the business and not just **In** the business as suggested by the graphic in *Figure 115*. The art is in balancing the evolution of systems and process maturity with its stage of evolution. Overly developed systems and processes can restrict change and constrain growth so need to be developed at a pace that matches the organization's ability to absorb and benefit from them.

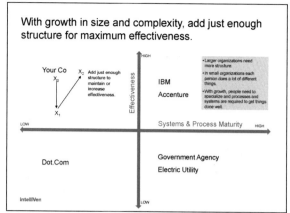

Figure 114. *Summary of how to manage effectiveness vs. maturity in the face of growth.*

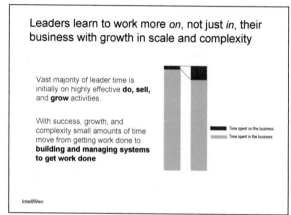

Figure 115. *Leaders learn to work more on, not just in, their organization in the face of growth in scale and complexity.*

EXERCISE 3: ORGANIZATION STUDY

Insert on the graphic to the right where your organization is and is headed.

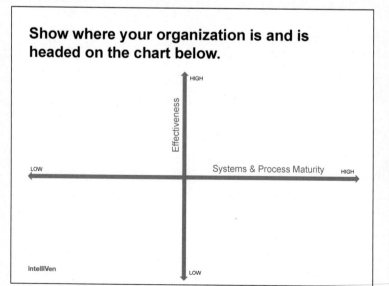

Figure 116. *Show where your organization is and is headed in terms of effectiveness and maturity.*

Summary

Use the *Manage to Lead* exercises, work problems, and templates to describe where the organization is, and where it is headed next, in terms of the actions driven by the seven truths as summarized below:

- **Get Clear**: Describe the organization in terms of whose problem it solves, how (as in how does it do, sell, and grow what it does), how well (compared to others, its past, and relative to its plan and projections. Lay out the P&L, cash flow, and balance sheet for the past two years, current four quarters, and two years hence.

- **Get Aligned**: Describe what kind of leader the one in charge has decided to be, who forms the core leadership team, and what leadership model is being used to collect followers aligned by a common understanding of where the organization is and a vision for where it is headed. Contract and govern each leadership team member's role and what the organization counts on from him/her.

- **Plan Change**: Describe what is most important to do differently next and the associated context for how it is today, why it needs to change, what things will be like when changed, and what will be hard about making the planned change.

- **Do & Review**: For every important thing the organization does (do, sell, grow); set goals, select performance metrics and target measures for each based on what the best do; predict what will happen, perform, observe, measure, compare, and determine what happened, why what happened was different than what was predicted, what there is to learn from that, and what will be different going forward. Make adjustments and repeat. Regularly review important initiatives, functions, clients, and prospects. Compare performance to plan and give guidance to those assigned to lead in their quest to make their "page of the plan".

- **Get Help**: Build and administer an accountability board and, separately, also build an advisory board of experts in what the organization does. Join a peer group. Retain a coach.

- **Focus:** Determine what is most important to do well and which of the most important personnel should be dedicated to achieving what is most important. Align for each team member what s/he wants to do, with what s/he is good at doing, and with what s/he likes doing that the organization needs him/her to do.

- **Grow:** Strive for scale along the three dimensions of operations: do, sell, and grow as the organization progresses from concept to start-up, credible, sustainable, and mature stages of evolution. Implement dashboards to guide execution and continuous development. Get help from those who have previously traveled the path you are on but implement only their suggestions which makes sense given the organization's stage of maturity to not drag down performance with premature development of systems and processes.

Package the elements from above and from all of the Organization Exercises to form a multi-year strategic plan that communicates how the organization views where it has been, where it is now, and where it is headed next and what it intends to do in order to get from where it is to where it is headed.

After a year striving to achieve the plan by implementing Managing to Lead the leader compares actual results with plan to study what happened, why what happened was different than plan, what is to be learned from that, and what to do differently going forward as a result. Repeating the process over several years and comparing actual to planned results year-to-year, empowers the leader to manage the organization to fulfill its potential to perform, and grow.

References

Blanchard, K. (1994). *Situational leadership.* Escondido CA: *Blanchard Training and Development, Inc.*

Bruch, H. & Walter, F. (2005). The keys to rethinking corporate philanthropy. *MIT Sloan Management Review.* 47 (1).

Catlin, K. & Matthews, J. (2001). *Leading at the speed of growth: Journey from entrepreneur to CEO.* New York: *Hungry Minds, Inc..*

Collins, Jim (2001). *Good to great: Why some companies make the leap…and others don't.* New York: Harper Collins.

Covey, S. (2004). *The 7 habits of highly effective people.* New York: Simon & Schuster.

Csikszentmihaly, M. (1990). *Flow: The psychology of optimal experience.* New York: Harper & Row.

Doyle, M. (1993). *How to make meetings work.* New York: Penguin.

Kotter, J. *8- Step change model: Implementing change powerfully and successfully.* Retrieved from: http://www.mindtools.com/pages/article/newPPM_82.htm

Lencione, P. (2002). *The five dysfunctions of a team: A leadership fable.* New York: Jossey-Bass.

Mindtools. *The wheel of life: Finding balance in your life.* Retrieved from: http://www.mindtools.com/pages/article/newHTE_93.htm

Gerber, M. *(1995). The e-myth revisited: Why most small businesses don't work and what to do about it. New York: Harper Collins.*

Harding, D. & Rovit, S. (2004). *Mastering the merger.* Boston: Harvard Publishing.

Hollander, D. (1991). *The doom loop system.* New York: Penguin Group.

Hrebiniak, L. (2005). *Making strategy work: Leading effective execution and change.* New Jersey: Pearson.

Ohmae, K. (1982). *The mind of the strategist: The art of Japanese business.* New York: McGraw-Hill.

Porter, M. (1996). *What is strategy? Harvard Business Review.* Retrieved from: http://hbr.org/product/hbr-s-10-must-reads-on-strategy-with-featured-arti/an/12601E-KND-ENG?referral=01622

Appendix

Executive Sessions

Executive Sessions are a way to provide extraordinarily rich input to leaders who seek to improve their own performance, the performance of their top teams, and of their entire organization. Presenting leaders find the process challenging, rigorous, and demanding.

The leader presents what s/he is working on and how it is going to two to five outside reviewers. The session objective is to get the leader and their top team on track to increasing the odds of more successful results sooner by having to prepare for the session, enhanced thinking and ideas that develop during the session, and from aggressive follow-up on the heels of the session.

Executive Sessions are not for leaders who are faint-of-heart. Leaders must come to the session prepared to learn new things, to have their current thinking challenged, and should allow themselves to be vulnerable and open to input. If a leader thinks they already know all they need to know and only wants to confirm that they are on the right track then they should not bother to attend an Executive Session.

The Executive Session format has evolved over 35 years through practical experience and application by highly successful business leaders across the country. It has been successfully administered hundreds of times with truly inspirational results.

INTRODUCTORY EXECUTIVE SESSION POAD

PURPOSE
Introduce a leader to:

- The rigors of consolidating what they are doing in order to share with an accountability board.

- The value of peer-review in a constructive and developmental forum.

- A clear path to a higher probability of a better result, sooner.

OUTCOMES

Hard Outcomes

- Management presentation of what the leader's organization is trying to do and how it is going.

- Insights, ideas, and action items from having prepared and presented the attached to a highly qualified and interested group of advisors and peers.

- Ideas as to how IntelliVen can provide immediate and sustained value to Guest CEOs business.

Soft Outcomes
- Leader:

  - Feels good about themselves, the work they did to prepare, and the value derived from presenting their material to the participants.

- Sees value from preparing for and working with this forum.

- Participants:

  - Have a good sense for the leader and their strengths, developmental potential, approach, weaknesses, uptake capacity, disposition, and their openness to input and to being vulnerable.

  - Enthusiasm for getting to know and to work further with the Leader and their top team.

APPROACH

Participants:

- Leader and members of the executive team as desired

- Lead reviewer

- 2-4 other reviewers

Preparation:

Leader:

- Reads background material notes on boards and on leadership through executive development

- Prepares five-or-so-page management overview presentation to describe:

  - What s/he is trying to do

  - What has been done to accomplish it

  - What happened

  - What has been learned so far

  - What s/he plans to do next

- Reviews material with lead reviewer ahead of the session to provide light guidance and feedback to increase the odds that the Executive Session goes well

Lead reviewer forwards presentation and other background material to the attendees a day or so before the session. It is important that materials are completed and distributed ahead of the session to give reviewers a chance to prepare, develop points of view, and formulate questions and begin to form ideas and suggestions to share. It is also important for the leader to step back from the micro focus of preparation to regain perspective and get ready to lead the session.

Session:

- Lead reviewer introduces the Leader and the participants and reviews the sessions objectives (10-15 minutes)

- Leader: (25-45 minutes)

  - Ensures participants have prepared material at hand or displays for all to see

  - Walks-through the material with the group

- Participants, each in turn: (25-45 minutes)

    - Ask questions, one at a time and in sequence, to clarify or probe further until time runs out or until questions are completed

    - Offer best advice based on what has been heard in the session

- Leader recapitulates what has been heard and thanks the group for their input and effort

DELIVERABLES

- Leader:

    - Works with their Lead Reviewer to consolidate insights, decisions, and action items from the session

    - Drafts and sends participants a note on what they got out of the session

- Participants:

    - Caucus to consolidate insights, and

    - Consider possible next steps

    - Decide recommended course

    - Communicate recommendations to Leader via Lead reviewer

- Arrange next steps as appropriate and desired by Leader; e.g.:

    - Future Executive Sessions

    - In-line operating support to operations, finance, marketing & sales, etc.

    - Project work (e.g., analysis, plan, budget, strategy, etc.)

Five Steps to Convert a Prospect into a Sale

Developing a systematic approach to cultivating demand for its products and services is a key step in the evolution of every successful organization. Many early-stage leaders long for a silver-bullet solution; that is, they look to hire someone with a lot of contacts and an extroverted personality to hit the market and drum up demand. Such efforts usually fail.

Leaders cannot count on building a scalable demand creation system by hiring one super-salesman after another. There are simply not enough to go around. A better strategy is to figure out for themselves how to create demand for their offerings and then hire and train others to follow their lead.

What follows is a sure-fire method for figuring out how to systematically turn prospects into customers that every executive, client manager, product manager, and sales professional can and should add to their tool set. It takes a lot of work to prepare properly and to execute well in a teaching-mindset, instead of a selling one, but those who are up to the task will be well-rewarded.

STEP-1: DESCRIBE WHAT YOU THINK YOUR PROSPECT IS TRYING TO ACCOMPLISH.

Use all the data about a top prospect you can get your hands on to describe what problem they seek to solve that your organization can help with. Arrange a face-to-face meeting with the person in charge of solving the problem and for whom solving it is strategic and who has the budget and business case to do so. After opening pleasantries ask the following question in a nice way: *"Would you like to know what I think you think is the most important thing you are trying to do?"*

You can be sure of a positive response because it is human nature for a person to want to know what someone else thinks they think. At the same time, no one expects you to be 100% correct. They might even chuckle inside at that thought that you could come close knowing what they think. As a result, your prospect is sure to be interested in hearing what you have to say, even if just for the entertainment value!

This gives you a safe opening to lay out your best articulation of what you think they are trying to do. The beauty of this approach is that to the extent you get it right you gain credibility and even if you get it wrong, you get credit for trying and you will almost always get helpful input to get it right! If you are right or reasonably close continue on to Step-2.

STEP-2: DESCRIBE WHAT OTHERS WHO HAVE DONE THE SAME FOUND DIFFICULT.

Resist the temptation to sell at this point. Do not talk about how hard or important it is for the prospect to do what they are trying to do. Doing so will invite resistance and cause the conversation to come to a grinding halt. Instead, talk about others to keep the conversation in a safe space and to invite the prospect to fully engage. Odds are s/he will lean forward and listen intently because you just might know what you are talking about and say something important.

Now is the time for you to make a good impression with a clear and articulate summary of what you know about the subject. Do not talk about your own organization or your products and services (i.e., resist the urge to start selling) and do not talk about the prospect's organization or problems. Focus the conversation on other organizations and what they have struggled with in a way that brings home just how hard it is to do this important thing well and that you know a great deal about how to do what needs to be done.

Sprinkle specific details about others with whom your prospect is likely to be familiar, and even better if the examples relate to their feared or hated competitors or to organizations the prospect admires and would like to emulate. While it does not matter in general if what you share comes from first-hand experience, from others you know or have worked with, or from case literature, it is more genuine and adds more to your credibility if it is clear that you have had personal involvement.

In addition to building credibility, the objective of this step is to confirm that your prospect does indeed have the problem you are prepared to solve. If you start by saying:

"Do you have problem X?"

You run the risk that the prospect is reluctant to share the truth. Instead, say:

"Organization A had problem X"

Thereby creating the opportunity for your prospect to volunteer:

"That's amazing…we have the same issue!"

The net effect is to build your credibility while drawing out important information for you to use later.

STEP-3: DESCRIBE HOW THE BEST HAVE SUCCEEDED.

Lay out the approach that the best use to accomplish what the prospect is trying to do. Odds are that they will be all ears as you help them see what important things they do not already know but that they could know if you were on their team. On the other hand, if it turns out that they are already know, and are already doing, what the best do then they may not be a good customer after all.

Here, too, mention how you have personally been involved in some of the "best" cases. There are only three things you have to sell: your company, your service or offering, and yourself. Selling yourself is the easiest and most important of the three and this is your chance to make that sale. Your competence, engaging approach, and evidence of your experience make or break the sale at this point.

STEP-4: DESCRIBE ALTERNATIVE COURSES OF ACTION.

Given what you know now about your client and what others have done, you are in position to share alternative courses of action that your prospect could follow. For example, they could continue as they were, they could try to figure out and follow best practices on their own, or they could work with a knowledgeable third party to navigate the course.

If what they are trying to accomplish is truly important and the stakes are high, they would be foolish to continue as they were. If it is hard to get it right on their own, then it should be an obvious decision to get outside help assuming outside help is available at a price that makes sense relative to the value of accomplishing the objective and the cost of failure.

They could look around for others to work with or they could work with you. Because you happen to be the one in front of them at that very moment, you are the one who helped them discover this opportunity, and because you are now brimming with credibility, it is the ideal time to share your approach to addressing the problem with high odds of landing a new customer with Step-5.

STEP-5: RECOMMEND NEXT STEPS.

Use your best judgment to recommend which of the alternatives they should follow. Lay out what they should do, what they should have you do or provide, and what value that leads to for their organization.

Make clear that this is an important part of what your organization does and that it would be an honor to turn them from a prospect into a customer and under what terms.

If the prospect says "no" to retaining you then it is time to start selling. As they say, selling begins when you hear the word "no"! Along the way try to learn the basis for their resistance so you can factor it into your approach for next time. On the other hand, if you hear: "yes" then you have made a sale by teaching and not by selling. Start to package what you have done and train others to so the same.

Below is an example of key points related to each of the five steps in a real example used by a firm that sold Program Management Office services to top government agencies.

Three Steps to Selling a Professional Services Work-Plan

Follow the three steps in this note to arrange a contract to provide professional services work for a client. Buyers of professional services work provided by outside contractors should also pay attention to these points.

To calculate a price for a body of work, a contractor first prepares a work-plan including tasks, assigned personnel, and the number of hours required to complete the work. The number of hours for each person is multiplied by their billing rate and summed to compute the price. When the contractor presents the work-plan and the price to the prospect, haggling ensues. The result is usually frustrating for both parties with the contractor getting a lower price for the same work-effort and the prospect feeling gouged.

The prospect wants the work at a price they can afford and the contractor wants a fair price given what it is going to take to get the work done. The problem is that they are in a tense situation, dealing from their own frame of reference, and trying to do too much to close the deal all in one step. Fortunately, there is a straightforward process to slow things down and, if followed to-a-tee, markedly increase the odds of a smooth progression to a signed contract.

Start with the list of the tasks required to accomplish a prospective client's specific objective. Then follow these three steps precisely to maximize the chance of landing a project to perform the work at target rates:

- **Agree on the tasks to be completed:** Arrange a time to sit down with your prospective client to review their objective, the value of achieving it, and each task required to secure it. Discuss each task thoroughly and without regard to who will perform the task and without any mention of price The focus at this point is entirely on what must be done to achieve the desired result and the enormous value of so doing. Get your prospect to add/change/delete tasks so that they develop a legitimate sense of ownership of the work-plan.

- **Agree on who will perform each task:** Once the work-plan is agreed to, review the resources required to perform each task to completion with excellence and how long it will take a qualified person to perform them. Point out that less qualified people will take longer and not do as good a job but will be less expensive per hour but do not dwell on price any more than that at this point in the process. Once you agree on the allocation of resources and durations proceed to step three.

- **Compute price:** Show the hourly billing rates for the selected resources, multiply by the hours required for each to perform tasks assigned to them and sum the result to calculate the total price of performing the complete set of tasks. If the client balks at the total price, remind them of the value they are getting by completing this work and point out that the cost is but a small fraction of that value. If there is still pushback on the price, go back to steps 1 and 2 and work with the client to decide which tasks do not really need to be performed at all or which can safely be performed by less qualified (and therefore also less expensive) staff. Your objective is to deal with price concerns by tinkering with tasks and resources and thereby adjusting total price by changing the scope and not just by getting paid less for the same work. You can sweeten the deal with a one-time credit if you like but it is best to NOT reduce hourly rates because once lowered it is near impossible to return to full hourly rate pricing whereas a one-time credit amount can more easily be granted or not on a case by case basis.

Prepare a separate exhibit for each of the three steps and go through them one at a time incorporating the edits from the preceding steps right then and there in the meeting as you proceed. If the edits are too extensive, stop the process and go back to the office, make changes to what has been covered, and arrange another time to meet again to complete the three steps.

Keep in mind that there is some specific value to the output of the effort. Review this early in the process so that, later, you can point out that the cost of doing the work is but a fraction of the value generated.

How marketing activities can cultivate a prospect to become a customer.

A good way to think about marketing is to consider it a four-stage process that goes from Prospect to Customer. Each stage has a program of marketing activities that move a prospect along the path to a sale.

Attract activities make a broad audience of possible prospective customers aware of the selling organization and promote its **Capture** activities. **Attract** activities include advertising, brochures, industry events, public speaking, published articles, press mentions, and mailings.

Capture activities increase a prospect's knowledge of the selling organization through a value-added relationship and tie directly to **Convert** activities. **Capture** activities typically are educational or research-focused, are offered by invitation only, and deliver real and unique value.

Capture activities usually involve regular meetings, such as webinars or seminars, for prospective buyers to meet with their peers in other organizations, including current clients and outside experts. The selling organization's sales executives administer and facilitate sessions to be sure they go well, to get input from customers and prospects that is fed back to other departments, and to identify the most likely next customers in order to "follow them home" and for whom to commence **Capture** activity.

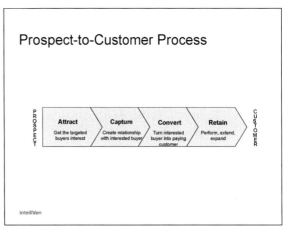

Figure 117. *Four steps turn a prospect into a customer.*

Capture activities are ongoing and provide an institutionally supported forum to hold and develop relationships with qualified prospects. **Capture** activities are aimed exclusively at qualified prospects unlike **Attract** activities which are aimed at broader audiences in hopes of appealing to the few qualified prospects that may be among them.

Capture activities are more like **Retain** activities that enhance existing relationships with clients but instead with qualified prospects. The theory being that if you treat a qualified prospect like a client soon they will become one. Invest in **Capture** activities exclusively with those in organizations you know you want to have as customers. The yield on such investments tends to be high and the input and feedback from listening to and interacting directly with clients and targeted prospects is invaluable.

Convert activities are sales efforts such as prospect visits, demonstrations, in-person meetings, reference checks, proposals, and lead tracking. The most important selling tool in this stage is a Point-of-View Sales Deck and associated script that present the important business problem that the selling organization solves, why it is hard to solve, what the best have done to solve it, alternative paths forward, and how the selling organization can best help (see: Five Steps to a Sale (http://www. intelliven.com/five-steps-to-convert-a-prospect-into-a-sale/)).

Retain activities support and cultivate the relationship that burgeons when value is delivered with the objective to cultivate a long-term, value-added relationship that ideally extends and expands without end. In addition to a program of periodic mailings, conversations and client events, clients are often invited to participate in **Capture** events to assist in influencing prospects perception of the firm and its work.

The bottom line is that **Attract** activities keep people busy but are far less likely to be productive than **Capture** activities which take a lot of high-end and focused effort but are worth every penny.

How to handle a disgruntled client

When you have a disgruntled client, there are three things to do in order to get things back on track:

Unload the negative: In a face-to-face meeting, first invite your client to inform you of all the things that are bothering him/her in great detail. Ask clarifying questions to draw out and completely understand exactly what the trouble is. It is very important to repeat back each point in order to get explicit confirmation that you understand exactly what has been said. It is equally important to avoid contradicting the client, imposing your views, or defending against what is being said in any way. This task is complete when the client has said everything that is on his/her mind and when you have recapitulated with a complete summary of all of the points that have been brought to your attention. While you may be itching to tell your side of the story and to correct any misinformation, stay calm, repress such urges, and stick with the guidance above. It takes great self-control to do, but just keep asking for more, and recapitulate again, until the client has no more to say and they are completely sure you have heard them accurately. The point here is that it will be a great deal easier for your client to hear and listen to you after they have been heard.

Transition to positive: In the same meeting, next establish a basis of trust and credibility with a forthright, honest and sincere apology for anything you have done wrong and a firm statement about your interest and intent to do what it will take to make things right. Every sword still in its sheath must be laid on the table so that there are no barriers between parties which would inhibit moving forward. Ask the client if they would like to hear your perspective on the same points just raised. If so, share your version of the facts. The objective is to create an atmosphere of mutual interest and understanding that leads naturally to a joint desire to move forward. If the client is not interested in your side of the story or if they refuse to imagine that there is anything you could do to get on track for success, then there is not much point in going further.

Take positive action: The third step in the same meeting is to make a concession so that your client feels they are getting something to make amends even if you still believe their claims have no merit. Then lay out and initiate actions that prove you are committed to moving forward and to make things right. Positive action, no matter how small, is absolutely vital to close out the meeting. The number one reason things go wrong is lack of management attention. Assure your client that you will stay involved in order to make sure things stay on track and their needs will be met. Then follow through by paying attention, staying in touch, and making sure things come out right.

Each of these three steps must be taken and worked through to completion in one session and in the order presented. To prepare for the session, compile the facts as you understand them so that in step one you can be listening to discover what they client knows or has experienced that you may not know and so that in the second step you have an organized, orderly and unemotional presentation of what you have to say. Be creative in step three. Find a way to give something in order to get something so that both parties feel that they have come out ahead and to lay the groundwork for a long and fruitful relationship.

How to increase the odds of success with a strategic acquisition or alliance.

Most acquisitions and alliances severely under-perform relative to expectations (http://www.langerco.com/lectures/acrobat_pdf/MA_Today.pdf)[1] set at the time of their inception. No matter how great they look on paper, it is always a lot harder to make things come out anywhere near where they were meant to be than it seemed at the start. Fortunately, based on first-hand practical experience and learning from experience of others, there are some things that can be done to raise the odds of success.

The reason for one organization to acquire or ally with another almost always boils down to one of the following three:

- To obtain **new products** and services to sell to existing customers.

- To secure access to **new customers** for existing offerings.

- To acquire needed **new resources** such as skills, leadership or knowledge.

There are also three basic reasons for one organization to decide NOT to acquire or ally with another:

- Most require the buyer to pay a premium price except in distressed situations in which case a bargain price is offset by high risk.

- Integration and assimilation of people, processes and systems is time-consuming and difficult. Time and effort spent to overcome cultural differences is enormous and rarely successful. Despite management's best intent, the wisdom of working together on the front-line is lost, without a lot of attention from the top, in favor of protecting turf, in-fighting, and favoritism.

- Acquisitions and alliances require alarmingly high concentrations of management attention to consider, plan, execute, launch, and nurture to success. Once the deal is done, even greater amounts of time from the most senior managers is required to plan and guide the integration of people, products, services and administrative processes which diverts management attention from other important matters.

There are three steps to successfully acquire or ally with another operation with the intent to merge it into existing operations (i.e., as opposed to operating as a separate unit):

- Determine whether the nature of the relationship between the two organizations is to be transactional, collaborative, innovative, or identity-shaping where who they are is literally defined by their relationship to each other.

- Develop a picture of the way things will work when operations come together as envisioned, including:

  - A multi-year financial plan that lays out the target financials which justifies the terms and to serve as the foundation for performance goals,

  - An operating model to show who will do what to deliver the joint entity's products and services with excellence, on time, and in budget; systematically and programmatically sell the venture's products and services; and develop its capacity to fuel growth, and

  - An organization and governance model to show who is responsible for doing (see: post on every top leader getting at least one thing right (http://www.intelliven.com/a-note-on-focus/)) and reviewing (see: post on connecting top leaders to the front-line (http://www.intelliven.com/note-on-reviews-to-connect-the-top-of-the-house-to-the-front-line/)) what initially and over time.

---

1   See for example: http://www.langerco.com/lectures/acrobat_pdf/MA_Today.pdf

- Assign leaders from both organizations to work together to identify issues, perform analysis and recommend actions consistent with the goals of the partnership. Success or failure to achieve targeted results must be a primary component to these individuals' personal performance assessment and bonus compensation for the performance period.

SUCCESS FACTORS

Experience shows that there are three important things that dramatically improve the probability that two organizations will be successful as partners in an alliance or acquisition:

- It must be clear to people, particularly the leaders, in each organization why they have decided to work together[1] (see Mastering the Merger (http://www.amazon.com/Mastering-Merger-Critical-Decisions-Break/dp/1591394384/ref=sr_1_fkmr3_1?ie=UTF8&qid=1339252543&sr=8-1-fkmr3&keywords=making+mergers+work+bain)). The rationale must be written down and shared with others in both organizations each from their own perspective and from the perspective of the other. For example, people in Organization A must be able to say why it makes sense for Organization B to have entered into the relationship as well as why it makes sense for their own organization to have done the same.

- The stakes must be high for both parties. Goal achievement must be highly rewarded. Conversely, lack of success must result in a significant negative impact to those involved.

- Each organization must assign a senior person to represent their interests. This individual needs to be a leader who personally stands to gain or lose a great deal both from a financial, and professional perspective depending on the fate of the venture. Their number-one goal is the success of the initiative. They serve as gateways to their respective organizations to facilitate the success for their counterpart who would otherwise be in a hopeless position of having to figure out for themselves how to work effectively in an alien organization. Therefore those assigned to this key role have to be senior, seasoned, well-regarded executives who can move mountains in their own organizations, if necessary, to make things work.

---

[1] See Mastering the Merger; http://www.amazon.com/Mastering-Merger-Critical-Decisions-Break/dp/1591394384/ref=sr_1_fkmr3_1?ie=UTF8&qid=1339252543&sr=8-1-fkmr3&keywords=making+mergers+work+bain

Alternatives to installing a Chief Operating Officer (COO) at lower cost and with higher odds of success.

The responsibilities shouldered by the successful Chief Executive Officer (CEO) increase with an organization's progress and growth in scale and complexity. The tension between the need to get things done, get others to do things, bridge the "white space" between organizational units, and to represent the organization externally (e.g. to investors, regulators, partners, suppliers, donors, the board, and the market) typically grows to the point where the CEO seeks to install a Chief Operating Officer (COO) in hopes of spreading the workload.

While adding a COO to the management team may be the right thing to do over the long term, it is a difficult, time consuming, expensive, and risky move that is not likely to pay off in the short-term because:

- The ideal candidate is rarely already 'in-house'. Those already in the organization are typically too vital in their current role, or not appropriate given their abilities and interests. Moving them into the role leaves too big a hole and may be too much like asking a rabbit to swim.

- The cost to find, recruit, hire, and on-board the ideal candidate from outside the organization is significant. It takes a long time, consumes precious management time, and is expensive both in terms of search fees and the incremental cost to compensate the new person.

- The odds of successfully bringing in someone from the outside are low. The failure rate of such placements is high because of how difficult it is to:

  - Bring a new senior player into an existing team of executives

  - Prepare an organization for a new COO

  - Support the new COO in getting up to speed and powerfully assuming the role

In light of the above it is a good idea to consider one of the two following alternative approaches.

THE DEPUTY

While the forward-thinking CEO can and should work on a long-term strategy, there is an alternate approach to installing a COO that creates short-term improvement that may be adequate for quite some time. The approach is to define a staff role to the CEO that facilitates and drives the management operating framework thereby offloading an enormous operating burden from the CEO. A person in such a role is often called a Deputy Senior Officer or a Chief of Staff and is common in military and government organizations and in organizations that serve governments, such as SAIC among others.

The Deputy position can be filled by someone with competencies that range from high-end administrative to those of a near-COO or even someone who could eventually someday serve as COO or CEO. The best strategy is to assign, from inside or hired-in, a low-ego, high-skilled person who is liked and non-threatening to the existing leaders and who is positioned for maximum benefit and long-term potential to the organization. The higher the skill level, the higher the price, the harder to find, and the more risk of sparks flying when existing leaders realize there is another strong(er) player in their midst.

THE ANALYST

An even less risky, less expensive, and more easily accomplished solution in the short-term is to fill the staff position with a business analyst that has:

- A high-bandwidth intellect with deep knowledge of any important part of the organization and who has interest and energy for all parts of the organization

- A lot of energy, capacity, and drive

- Ability to conceptualize and articulate an accurate big picture from a myriad of details and to communicate complex concepts even to those who are not conceptual

- Acumen for management and leadership

- A disposition that is compatible with the CEO

- A "long runway"; i.e., early in their career, bright, and an ambitious person who is likely to go far.

Assigning top business analysts to staff roles is common to organizations such as IBM, Apple, and Motorola where top-flight young professionals, often graduates of top business schools with just a few years of experience, are assigned as Executive Assistants to the organization's top executives for a year or two before returning to other roles in the organization. The executives get extraordinary service and the up-and-coming assistant gets a front-line education and opportunities to grow and perform that are unsurpassed.

To increase the odds of having such talent on staff, hire MBAs fresh-out of the top schools and groom them in the business for a few years and then assign the best to staff top executives as described. On the other hand, the best MBAs have probably been courted and brought on by top consulting firms. Consequently, a shortcut is to find and retain a business analyst from a top firm on a consulting basis to work full-time in the Analyst role for a top executive. If they work out well, hire them as employees. If not, place them elsewhere or cycle them back to where they came from and try again.

> The author very successfully followed this exact strategy as the top executive at Hyperion Software in the late '90s with a Harvard MBA retained from a top consulting firm.

SUMMARY

With either approach the course of action is to define the role, conduct a search, and then design and drive a process to work with the alternative to the COO, the CEO, and the management team to bring them on board and to get everyone on track for success.

How to run a great annual Leadership Team Strategy Offsite Meeting.

PURPOSE

The purpose of the **Annual Leadership Team Offsite** is for organization leaders to break away from day-to-day operations in order to:

- **Celebrate successes** in the year ending.

- Review, discuss, and refresh their **alignment on where the organization is headed** and why it is headed there, **performance against goals** over the past year, and to lay the **foundation for performance targets and strategic initiatives** for the coming year.

For Leadership Team members to:

- Be directly exposed to, and to effect, the thinking of the CEO and the Core Leadership Group.

- Get to know each other better and to **develop as a team**.

- Bounce ideas off of each other to reach **new insights and paths** forward.

- Identify and work on key issues that cross organization boundaries.

OUTCOMES

Hard Outcomes:

- Leadership Team aligned around vision, **perception of operating performance relative to plan, assessment of progress on Strategic Initiatives, and guiding parameters** for the coming year's plan and initiatives.

- Preliminary cut at a list of **Strategic Initiatives** for the coming year.

- First look at bottom-up **performance prospects** for the coming year.

- **Insights, action items, and decisions** reached during the session.

Soft Outcomes:

- Leadership Team understands and is aligned with, and in support of, the leader's vision, strategies, strategic initiatives, and next steps.

- Team members are:

  - **Excited to be part of the organization** and its Leadership Team.

  - In agreement about where the organization is heading and confident that it can get there.

  - **On board and ready to think and act** day-to-day in ways that are aligned with the leader, each other, the organization's vision, operating plan, strategic initiatives, goals and with the way leaders have decided to behave.

  - **Accepting ownership** of "Their Page of the Plan". I.e. each leader knows, understands and believes in his/her role in achieving the vision and has a burning desire to contribute to the team's overall success.

  - Confident that the leader and team members know, like, appreciate, respect and admire them; that they are being counted on and can meet or beat performance expectations.

- Satisfied that their **views have been listened to and heard** by the leader and the Leadership Team.
- Accepting the process as important and valuable.
- Convinced that the leader and leadership team are **acting in accord with organization core values**.
- Know who is in vs. out; who among them are growing and what new skills need to be brought on to the team through development of existing members or by adding new members
- Fully **considerate of input** from the Board, Leadership Team, and staff.

APPROACH

PRE-MEETING		
ITEM	**RESPONSIBLE PERSONS**	**STEPS**
Planning	CEO, Core Leaders, Facilitator	Facilitator drafts Purpose, Outcomes, Approach, and Deliverables; iterates with CEO who iterates further with Core Leaders and Leadership Team. Identify session topics, time slots, and session leaders.
Preparation	Session Leaders	**CEO meets briefly one-on-one with each presenter to give guidance** on what to prepare for their area or topic.
Pre-meeting reviews	Presenters, CEO, and Facilitator	**CEO and Facilitator meet substantively with each presenter to review what they will present** and to: • **give guidance** • **ensure that each is clear and aligned** with respect to the organization as a whole and with their area of responsibility. • **give feedback and push-up leader's thinking and material.** There should be no surprises; the CEO coaches and works with each leader to help ensure that each does well what the CEO is counting on them to do.
Collect board input	CEO, Core Leadership Team, Facilitator, Board	CEO presents to the board: • Where current year is likely to end up in terms of key performance metrics. • Summary of performance on Strategic Initiatives. • Top-down estimate of key performance metrics for coming year. Discuss to clarify and get guidance.
Prepare attendees	CEO, Facilitator, Leadership Team	Distribute this **POAD** to attendees and ask each to give thought to questions and topics that will be addressed at the session including: **"What are they most proud of having accomplished and what is most important to work on next?"** Functional, unit leaders, and topic researchers prepare briefs and review with CEO (as described above). **CEO prepares introductory briefing and reviews with Core Leaders and facilitator.**

DURING MEETING

TIME	LEADER	TOPIC
15 minutes	CEO	**Enthusiastically welcomes management team and reviews agenda & ground-rules.** (Note that the feel, tone, and visible energy of the opening sequence matter much more than exactly what is said. **See how to facilitate post (http://www. intelliven.com/how-to-be-a-good-group-facilitator-to-help-your-organization-and-to-grow-as-a-leader-when-the-opportunity-presents-itself/).)**
20-40 minutes	CEO	Presents concise, consolidated update on: • Where the organization has come from, where it is now, and where it is headed next and over the long term. Note that the opening is an opportunity to **manifest** (i.e., literally to bring to life) the very **essence of leadership** in that it is literally what it means for a leader to be a leader when he or she presents to the top team a vision, secures their alignment, and motivates them to act. • **Current year top initiatives and high-level summary of progress on each.** Note that it is important for the leader to be honest about where things have gone well and where things have not gone so well. Opens up for questions and comments.
Pre-meeting reviews	CEO	Asks Leadership Team members to share what they are most proud of having accomplished in the year now ending. Scribe, step-back and take a moment of pride in what has been shared. Asks Leadership Team members to share what they are most **looking forward to working on in the upcoming year.** Step-back and examine the list. Consolidate and streamline as appropriate. Note which items appear to be most important.
BREAK		

20 minutes presentation;20 minutes discussion for each	Functional and Unit Leaders	Each presents:
		
		• Key goals for the year now ending.
		  • What was done to reach them?
		  • What happened?
		  • What was learned?
		• What is planned to be done next; including
		  • Key initiatives and high-level financial performance measures for the next three years?
		  • What has to happen for these measures to be met?
		  • What are the risks that what has to happen will not happen and how will those risks be mitigated?
		
		Note that this section of the agenda puts each member of the Leadership Team in a position to be accountable for what they were to do and on the hook for future performance in front of their peers.
		
		CEO models how the group is to behave. Honor and respect speakers but **ask good questions to** push up thinking and to push back on ideas.
		
		Once things are rolling the CEO should hold their voice until towards the end of each round so as to create space for the team to work together.

DURING MEETING

TIME	LEADER	TOPIC
5 minutes	CEO and/or Facilitator	Open up the discussion calling for clarifying questions and then best advice.
20-40 minutes	CEO and/or Facilitator	After all have gone, step-back to identify and discuss key cross-cutting items that may have fallen through the cracks.

20 minutes presentation;20 minutes discussion for each	Topic experts or case leaders	Key topics and cases stories
		
		• Present:
		    • Key findings on emerging topics (such as key content areas researched ahead of the session; e.g., evolving world, technology, and economic trends); and
		    • Cases from operating experience that exemplify target behaviors and/or results.
		• Open the floor for additional input and to consolidate insights and implications.

Insert breaks as needed based on how many topics of each sort are to be covered; Insert group activities, and evening fun before, during, and after dinner	All	While the ropes course and trust-falls ARE the business, it is still important to get out and walk about in the open air as a group.
	CEO	Wrap up with warm appreciation for work performed, summary of key insights, decisions, and action items including what will be done by whom in follow up to the sessions

POST-MEETING

ACTION ITEM	RESPONSIBLE PERSONS	APPROXIMATE TIMING
Map out Operating Plans and Strategic Initiatives, risks, mitigation strategies, and resource needs and review with Core Leadership Team.	Functional and Unit leaders, Core Leadership Group	By end of September
Share assessment of prior performance period and suggested upgrades to Vision, Strategy, Operating Plan, and Strategic Initiatives with staff.	Functional and Unit Leaders	By Sep 30
Finalize high-level budget guidance.	CEO, CFO	By Sep 30
Finalize top company goals/targets.	Core Leadership Team	By Sep 30
Review preliminary Vision, Strategy, Operating Plan, Strategic Initiatives, and Performance Goals with Board.	CEO, Core Leadership Team, Board	End of October Board Meeting
Present updated Vision, Strategy, Operating Plan, and Strategic Initiatives to Board for approval.	CEO, CFO	Mid-December Board Meeting

DELIVERABLES:

- Recommended upgrades to corporate: Vision, Mission, Purpose, and Strategy,
- Preliminary list of Strategic Initiatives for the coming performance period,
- Input and suggested action items for functional and unit leaders,
- First cut at annual financial budget for the coming period.

How to run successful Operating Meetings

It is not hard to run an organization better…but you do have to work at it. Every meeting needs to be thought through to get clear why it is being held, what it is to produce, how it will be accomplished, and what outcomes are to be generated (see: How to Run a Great Meeting (http://www.intelliven.com/notes-and-tips-on-how-to-have-a-great-meeting/)). A good approach for Operating Group Meetings is for the organization's leader (e.g., CEO, unit leader, initiative leader, or project manager) to have each functional leader (e.g., head of engineering, head of marketing, etc.) present in literally just a few minutes:

- An update on open items from the prior meeting

- Key matters for the coming period

- What is needed from top management and other functional areas to perform well this period

- Any special "heads-up", critical questions or key concerns for the coming period

For each area there is a one-page handout (see **Key Items Tracking** below) that summarizes metrics, action items completed and open from last meeting, and a summary of the key items for the coming week. The meeting's administrative support person, or an electronic central repository, stores the summaries and displays them, or hands them out ahead to be at-hand during the meeting.

The entire group engages briefly, and briskly, as needed on each area in turn. Ground rules guide behavior and help team members operate as a collective leadership (i.e., what can each of us do to help the entire organization operate as well as it possibly can) and committed to problem-solving (i.e., work the point not the person).

Core Leaders, including the COO, President, and CEO, also present what is on their respective lists for the week in the same meeting though it may be best for them to go last so as not to upstage others. When all have gone, the meeting is adjourned. The entire meeting should take about an hour and everyone should leave full of energy to attack what is on their plate to get done next.

Action Items are the responsibility of those who have them. They and their manager make sure they are completed. The meeting's administrative support person tracks them in a central repository (http://www.intelliven.com/note-on-meeting-records/) updated after the meeting and over the course of the week as items are completed.

Key Items Tracking: Each functional leader is responsible for his/her entire area. Within each area there are likely a select few items of keen interest that its leader tracks and speaks to at Operating Group Meetings. Of particular interest in addition to key performance indicators (http://en.wikipedia.org/wiki/Performance_indicator)[2] will be:

Items of significance because of associated **risk, potential leverage, or impact** on the rest of the organization,

- Items that **bridge between** responsibility areas

- Items of potential **risk or weakness** that have a good chance of occurring and a significant negative impact if they do and so must be mitigated against

- Items that fall off-track in terms of **schedule, cost, or quality**

Each leader maintains a display of the key items s/he is tracking that is forwarded to attendees, via the meeting's administrative support person or a central repository, prior to each meeting. The list lets the leader know what each member thinks the group is counting on from him or her.

---

2 See: http://en.wikipedia.org/wiki/Performance_indicator.

If what the meeting member thinks the leader and the group are counting on from him or her is not correct, the leader and the group's members provide feedback and guidance. An advance look at what will be presented by each area leader also triggers discussion, questions, corrections, updates, and constructive action all **prior** to the meeting even starting.

During the meeting, attendees are also encouraged to:

- Share relevant **new information**
- Ask for **clarification**
- Help to figure out **who owns following up** (perhaps full RASCI (http://www.valuebasedmanagement. net/methods_raci.html) or at least just R)
- Agree on **insights, decisions, action items, next steps and timing**

If someone thinks they want to say something, ask them first to verify that what they have in mind falls into one of the categories listed, otherwise it might not be necessary and increases the risk of prolonging the meeting and diminishing its effectiveness.

Along these lines, do not use the Operating Group Meeting to "work" issues or to discuss philosophy, mission, vision, culture, and the like. Use the Operating Group Meeting to inform and get on track to do what is needed in the coming period (e.g., week). If something needs to be "worked", time to do so is scheduled for the appropriate people including whoever is to take the lead and be sure the proper preparation takes place ahead-of-time.

In-between meetings, the leader meets one-on-one with each Operating Group member to talk more broadly about actions taken, results, how things are going, and what is to be done next in the member's realm of responsibility.

Effective leaders delegate responsibility for broad areas to specific Operating Group members while also tracking specific items in each area. If tracked items tend go well, then the Operating Group member gets a "checkmark", adds to the level of trust they have with the leader (and their peers), and they get more "rope". If tracked items do not go well, the leader probes further to see what else is wrong and where help and development might be needed.

At least twice each year the CEO calls for a full review of each functional area to see how it is performing relative to plan, progressing on its strategic initiatives, and laying the groundwork for next year's performance plan. Topics related to mission, vision, culture, purpose, and the like, are fodder for annual strategy offsite sessions often conducted over a two-day period (to be covered in a future post).

Sample Board of Directors Charter

Board of Directors		
Members	**Frequency**	**Responsibilities**
Internal Members Chairman CEO Secretary **External Members** Senior Advisor Managing Director Past CEO of similar organization **Inside Observers** CTO CFO Chief Marketing Executive **Outside Observers** Investor Banker	Every 2 Months and as needed	• Hires/Fires the CEO • Reviews and approves annual financial plan, option program, compensation program, and incentive program • Provides a consistent point of accountability for performance against plan and goals • Approves performance goals, compensation, incentives for firm's C-level executives • Reviews performance annually and guides the development of the CEO • Reviews and provides guidance with respect to what the firm and its top executives are doing individually and collectively, how it is going, what they are learning, and what they will do next • Provides guidance with respect to individual and collective executive focus • Reviews resources (people, clients, time, training, connections, money, etc.) needed to achieve plans and takes steps to help the firm meet its needs • Gets clear about what is most important, and ensures that enough attention is being paid to it • Reviews the firm's strategy and key initiatives to be sure they make sense and that they are in synch with what the firm is doing and learning • Provides direct advice and council in all communications and affairs relating to bankers and financiers

Sample Advisory Board Charter

SAMPLE
CHARTER FOR THE ADVISORY BOARD
OF
SOFTWARE SYSTEMS, INC.

PURPOSE:

The purpose of the Advisory Board (the "Advisory Board") established pursuant to this charter is to provide advice and otherwise satisfy requests from the chief executive officer (the "CEO") of Software Systems, Inc., a Virginia corporation (the "Company"), and its affiliates regarding any issues related to the Company and its affiliates that the CEO may present to the Advisory Board.

The Advisory Board will undertake the specific responsibilities listed below and will not have the authority or power to undertake any acts or duties except as the CEO may from time to time prescribe. For the avoidance of doubt, except as specifically authorized by the CEO in writing, neither the Advisory Board nor its individual members shall be authorized to bind the Company in any way or provide recommendations to the CEO.

MEMBERSHIP:

The Advisory Board shall consist of a minimum of one or more members as is determined by the CEO. The member(s) of the Advisory Board shall be appointed by and serve at the discretion and pleasure of the CEO. The Company shall establish the compensation of each member of the Advisory Board.

RESPONSIBILITIES:

The responsibilities of the Advisory Board include providing advice to the CEO regarding any issues related to the Company that the CEO may present to the Advisory Board, which may include programs, products and services of competitors and potential customers of the Company and its affiliates, the business development and marketing strategy of the Company and its affiliates, and the overall business plan of the Company and its affiliates.

MEETINGS:

Meetings of the Advisory Board may be held at such time and place as shall from time to time be determined only by the CEO.

Software Systems Advisory Board

Proposed Heads of Agreement with [_____]

[Month Day, Year]

Software Systems Objective:

To form an Advisory Board made up of 3 to 4 well-connected, external people who consistently over time:

- Add credibility in the federal government,

- Provide insight into business development and product development initiatives, and

- Help with networking, door-opening, and influencing with key customers, prospective customers, and partners.

Terms:

- Software Systems will:

    - Grant you options that will be worth approximately $100,000 if Software Systems achieves its base goals (i.e., realized valuation of 3 times invested capital) with corresponding upside if actual performance exceeds target. Options vest over 4 years and expire twelve months after termination.

    - Pay you $1500 (plus modest travel expenses) per Advisor Meeting.

    - Memorialize this agreement in a written contract.

- Advisors will:

    - Prepare for (i.e., read advance materials) and attend 3-4 Advisor Meetings per year.

    - Stay attentive and interested in Software Systems and what we do, our partners, competitors, customers and prospects.

    - Initiate contact to let us know anything that comes up that you think we would benefit from knowing.

    - Be available and interested to help top Software Systems leaders via phone, e-mail, and occasionally in-person on a spot basis.

    - Provide additional consulting support on an hourly basis at $250/hour ($2000/day) upon request of the CEO as your time and interest in so doing permits.

- Term is 2 years with automatic annual renewal; either party can terminate at any time and for any reason with 30-days written notice.

Agreed to by:_____   Agreed to by:_____

Title_____   Title_____

Date_____   Date_____

Why growth is good and money matters even in non-profit organizations and in support roles sought to avoid the seamy side of business.

Some students preparing to enter the work force and some early-stage professionals launching their career seek lines of pursuit that steer clear of what they believe to be the seamy, cut-throat, greedy world of business.

A course of study in, for example, Organization Development that leads to a career in Human Resources for a non-profit, government, education, or health organization seems like a path in which one might earn a living and have a positive impact on the world while avoiding matters related to money and growth. Even for those in support roles and for organizations not known for profit, however, **growth is good** and **money matters!**

With growth (see *Figure 118*) an organization that does good can do it on a **larger scale** and have even **greater impact**; offer employees **opportunities** to do **new and different things** often with greater scope and scale of responsibility and so also at **higher levels of compensation**; and generate societal lift from the **new jobs** it creates, **taxes it pays**, and the platform it offers for **community leaders** to emerge, all in addition to the possibility of **wealth creation** in some cases. Without growth an organization stagnates, its employees get bored doing the same thing year after year at the same level of pay and eventually leave for a more exciting opportunity elsewhere.

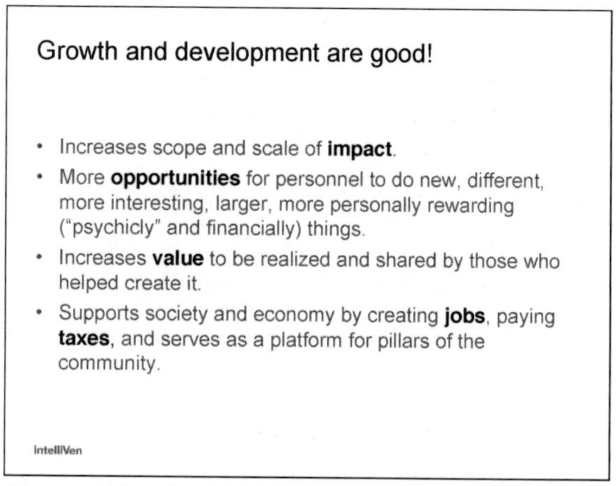

Growth and development are good!

- Increases scope and scale of **impact**.
- More **opportunities** for personnel to do new, different, more interesting, larger, more personally rewarding ("psychicly" and financially) things.
- Increases **value** to be realized and shared by those who helped create it.
- Supports society and economy by creating **jobs**, paying **taxes**, and serves as a platform for pillars of the community.

IntelIVen

Figure 118. *Growth is Good*

Money to organizations, including non-profits, that seek to grow in order to have a greater impact, create the opportunity for those who work there to do new things, spawn more jobs, and groom leaders to help a town, city, or state, is like the **gas in a car**. Without gas, a car stops running. An organization that does not think about, manage, and make ever more money, increases the odds that it will run out of fuel, cease to grow and, possibly, even to exist.

An aversion to, or fear of, numbers, dollars, and analytic thinking may mask a lack of confidence, energy, and drive; or provide a convenient hiding place in the name of idealism for those who simply do not want to work too hard.

Those in hiding may wonder about the wisdom of their strategy to steer clear of issues related to organization growth and money matters once they lean-into their discomfort and think through whether or not they personally plan to ever retire and, if so, how they plan to fund their living without an annual income.

Things start out simply enough. After graduation from college industrious students get a job, work hard, get paid, spend on goods and services, and save the rest as suggested by *Figure 119*. Savings, 401k contributions, pension, IRAs, profit from the sale of equity interests, inheritances, gambling winnings, and the like all contribute to an ever growing nest-egg to cover living costs when the decision is made to stop working.

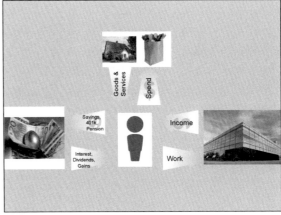

Figure 119. *Working generates income to cover expenses and feed savings.*

After what seems at first to be an eternity, the time eventually arrives when it would be nice to stop working and enjoy the fruits of a career's worth of labor. The question is: "How much wealth does one need to accumulate over the course of a career to finance living once s/he stops working?" The answer depends both on the rate of spending and on the financial returns realized on what is saved.

If one plans to never stop working, then living continues to be financed by work and significant savings may not be necessary. While working forever may be the only option for some, it eventually becomes infeasible due to infirmaries that come with age at which point perhaps there is a family member to live with or maybe it will be possible to live off the state or on the street. These may be good back-up options but likely not the first choice for most.

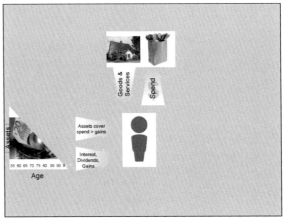

Figure 120. *Assets drawn down to cover expenses.*

Another option is to draw down accumulated assets (savings, 401k contributions, pension, IRAs, etc.) to cover spending for the remaining years of life. The problem is that if life turns out to be long (which is, of course, the preferred scenario!) the nest-egg might run out as suggested by the graphic in *Figure 120*.

With enough assets the nest-egg never gets smaller because annual gains from interest, dividends, and appreciation are greater than or equal to the sum of: annual spending, taxes associated with realized gains, and inflation. Whether one ever actually stops working or not, there is comfort in knowing there is no longer a need to work in order to finance living. That is, enough assets have been accumulated to achieve financial independence (http://en.wikipedia.org/wiki/Financial_independence) as suggested by the equilibrium demonstrated in *Figure 121*.

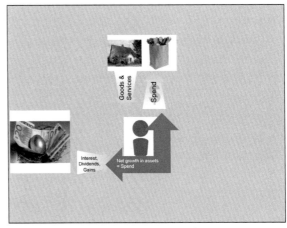

Figure 121. *Annual gains cover living expenses.*

A generation or two ago, many employers put away funds to payout to long-time employees in their later years in the form of a pension. Some teachers, government workers, and assembly-line workers, and many others might have made what seemed like less along the way but in retirement they are in great financial shape thanks to fully funded pensions. Pensions are far less common now. Some are under-funded (http://www.nytimes.com/2012/07/21/business/pension-plans-increasingly-underfunded-at-largest-companies.html?_r=1&) in that the amount put away is not enough to cover planned payments which can cause their organizations to go bankrupt (http://www.reuters.com/article/2012/08/02/us-usa-sanbernardino-debt-idUSBRE8711YU20120802).

Most employers now leave it up to each employee to provide for their own retirement. Many contribute to employee 401k and TIAA CREF savings plans including matching funds put in by employees after some number of months of service and up to an annual maximum. Employer contributions often vest according to years of service so be mindful when leaving to set departure dates in order to capture as much vesting as possible. Such contributions are a most welcome benefit in that they provide real money to help meet long-term financial needs but far from enough to ever secure financial independence.

Figure 122 shows what assets are required to indefinitely finance various levels of living under the assumptions presented above. Use a web-based financial independence number calculator (http://dvogelsang.blogspot.in/2012/04/calculating-your-financial-independence.html) to determine what assets are required to finance living under various assumptions about living expenses, tax rate, inflation rate, years to finance, and market performance.

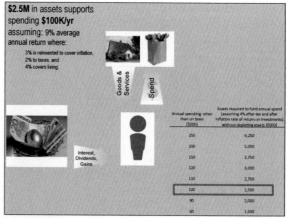

Figure 122. *Assets needed to cover various levels of annual expense.*

As shown in the model, to finance living costs indefinitely assuming annual expenses of $100,000, an average of 3% inflation per year, and 4% for taxes requires $2.5 M in assets invested in a balanced fund (see: Sustainable Withdrawals High Net Worth White Paper December 2011 (http://www.intelliven.com/wp-content/uploads/2012/12/Sustainable-Withdrawals-High-Net-Worth-White-Paper-December-2011.pdf)). Also shown is that $2 M in assets will be drained within 10 years with the same assumptions for taxes and inflation and $150,000 in annual living expenses.

Financial independence, once achieved, ensures that at life's end the portfolio of assets can be used to cover extraordinary medical costs that may occur or, better yet, left behind either to pass on to heirs or donate to chosen causes.

Growth is good and money really does matter. Each of us needs to sort out how they plan to cover costs of living upon retirement. Follow the recommendations in *Figure 123* to get on track to financial security.

See suggested additional readings in *Figure 124* for additional insight on matters related to managing personal finances and investments. For personal financial planning assistance see your financial adviser or contact The Mason Companies (http://www.masoncompanies.com/).

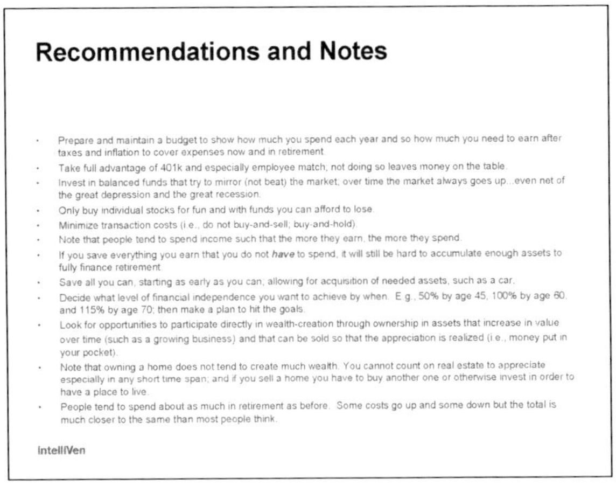

Recommendations and Notes

- Prepare and maintain a budget to show how much you spend each year and so how much you need to earn after taxes and inflation to cover expenses now and in retirement.
- Take full advantage of 401k and especially employee match; not doing so leaves money on the table.
- Invest in balanced funds that try to mirror (not beat) the market; over time the market always goes up...even net of the great depression and the great recession.
- Only buy individual stocks for fun and with funds you can afford to lose.
- Minimize transaction costs (i.e., do not buy-and-sell; buy-and-hold).
- Note that people tend to spend income such that the more they earn, the more they spend.
- If you save everything you earn that you do not *have* to spend, it will still be hard to accumulate enough assets to fully finance retirement.
- Save all you can, starting as early as you can; allowing for acquisition of needed assets, such as a car.
- Decide what level of financial independence you want to achieve by when. E.g., 50% by age 45, 100% by age 60, and 115% by age 70; then make a plan to hit the goals.
- Look for opportunities to participate directly in wealth-creation through ownership in assets that increase in value over time (such as a growing business) and that can be sold so that the appreciation is realized (i.e., money put in your pocket).
- Note that owning a home does not tend to create much wealth. You cannot count on real estate to appreciate especially in any short time span; and if you sell a home you have to buy another one or otherwise invest in order to have a place to live.
- People tend to spend about as much in retirement as before. Some costs go up and some down but the total is much closer to the same than most people think.

IntelliVen

Figure 123. *Recommendations and Notes related to managing personal financials.*

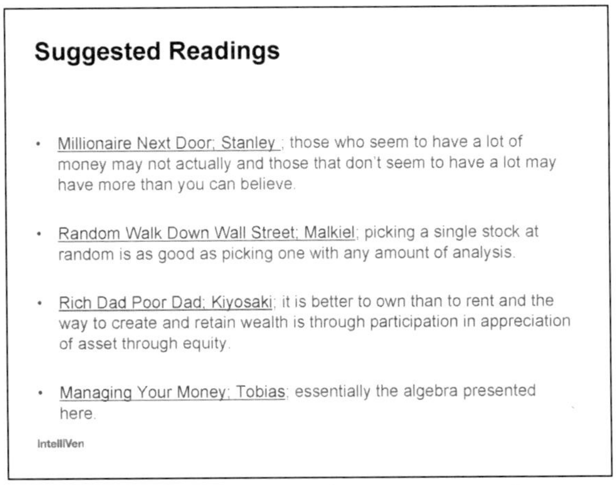

Suggested Readings

- Millionaire Next Door; Stanley ; those who seem to have a lot of money may not actually and those that don't seem to have a lot may have more than you can believe.

- Random Walk Down Wall Street; Malkiel; picking a single stock at random is as good as picking one with any amount of analysis.

- Rich Dad Poor Dad; Kiyosaki; it is better to own than to rent and the way to create and retain wealth is through participation in appreciation of asset through equity.

- Managing Your Money; Tobias; essentially the algebra presented here.

IntelliVen

Figure 124. *Additional readings on personal financial management.*

How to increase the odds of being happy and of leading a fulfilled life.

Most of us seek in our professional affiliation what some call a state of flow or what others call happiness, exhilaration, satisfaction, or fulfillment. Along these lines see: Flow: The Psychology of Optimal Experience (http://books.google.co.in/books?hl=en&lr=&id=v2AVz3gf-F4C&oi=fnd&pg=PT11&dq=flow+the+psychology+of+optimal+experience&ots=qG2dh1Bsau&sig=ahjkWIejpOc1fO-X0zDPZ4XfXu4&redir_esc=y#v=onepage&q=flowthe psychologyofoptimalexperience&f=false) by Mihaly Csikszentmihalyi (http://www.amazon.com/Mihaly-Csikszentmihalyi/e/B000AQ1KVM/ref=sr_ntt_srch_lnk_1?qid=1325875435&sr=8-1) and The Doom Loop System (http://www.amazon.com/Doom-Loop-System-Dory-Hollander/dp/067084229X) by my long time personal executive coach Dr. Dory Hollander who told me and others that the secret to a fulfilled life could be summarized in just four words (which are shared at the end of this post!).

Job satisfaction, however, may in the end not be something you can pursue for its own sake. It may, rather, be something that comes about as a by-product when you try hard to accomplish something. The best moments occur when body and/or mind are stretched to the limit in a voluntary effort to accomplish something difficult and worthwhile.

When in a state of such exertion and accomplishment, there is a sense of pride and fulfillment that is both pleasurable and addictive. Some who experience flow when climbing mountains scale a peak only to start preparing to climb the next even before leaving the summit and are doomed to repeat the experience over and over in a never-ending quest to bag the ultimate peak.

Many find something similar in their work lives when they lose themselves in a strong-minded pursuit of one single, all-consuming work goal after another, much like the mountain climber in search of the perfect peak.

While the career-minded person and the mountain climber may accomplish a great deal, their one dimension of focus might really be a copout. They have made life's most important decision too simple. That is, whenever there are tradeoffs between spending time in their area of focus and spending time on other things, the all-important quest compels them to always defer to their main line of pursuit.

The downside is that their success and fulfillment likely comes at great expense to family, friends, and ultimately also to themselves. Work and work goals are important but only as one dimension of a life.

On their death beds, some who accomplished a great deal in life but had shallow lives outside of work reveal that every step of the way they always did what they thought they had no choice but to do or what they truly believed was right to do. Only after it was too late did they realize they could have chosen to spend time in other areas of life and been happier.[3]

A more enlightened approach is to view work and work goals as important but only as one dimension of a multi-faceted life. Those who climb mountains, for example, might always look forward to the next climb but also have goals and aspirations along other lines including family, school, civic, social, sports, and the like.

A way to think about it is in the form of a spider diagram or Life Wheel (http://www.mindtools.com/pages/article/newHTE_93.htm), as depicted in *Figure 125 and 126*, where a person is seen to manage an ever evolving portfolio of pursuits throughout his/her life. They set milestones and goals in each line of pursuit and monitor progress. At any time they have consciously decided which of these are of top importance and so get the majority of time and attention. When the time is right, they switch emphasis to another.

The "quality of the journey" across the portfolio of pursuits, then, is revealed by the pattern of progress, actualization and recollection along all lines of pursuit — not just by how well things are going at work or on the mountain trail.

To pull this off, for each line of pursuit it helps to:

- Have a specific, hard-to-reach but achievable goal

- Inform others of your goals to inspire personal accountability to achieve them

- Work hard to reach the goal

- Know what to watch to know where you are in terms of reaching it

- Know you have, or will get, the skills and resources to be successful

- Enjoy it so much that you lose track of time in its pursuit

- Act intentionally on a chosen dimension to achieve a specific next stage of development

- Focus on just one or two or three at any point in time because it is hard to make much progress on more than one or two pursuits at a time and pursuing many paths at the same time results in thrashing and in being busy but with little progress

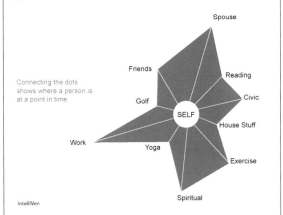

Figure 125. Personal Pursuits

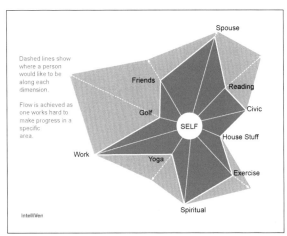

Figure 126. Personal Growth

---

3 See, for example, Gordon Livingtston's: Too Soon Old, Too Late Smart (http://www.amazon.com/Too-Soon-Old-Late-Smart/dp/1569244197): Thirty True Things You Need to Know Now.

- Concentrate on one or two or three for a specific period and then switch to another one or two at another time as feels appropriate. For example, in your mid-20s to late 30s you may focus on career and family then, in your 50s and 60s, work on travel, health, handicap, and giving back.

Along these lines, someone once said that the secret to a happy and fulfilled life can be summed up in just four words: **Act Intentionally … Persist Variously!**

WORK PROBLEM

Draw a picture like the one in *Figure 127* for yourself now and then add where you would like someday to be for each prong of your life:

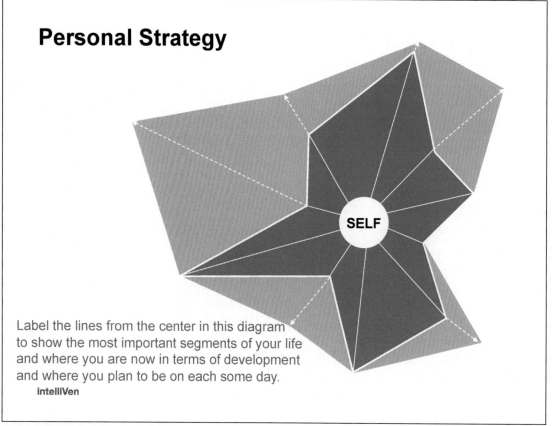

Personal Strategy

Label the lines from the center in this diagram to show the most important segments of your life and where you are now in terms of development and where you plan to be on each some day.
intelliVen

Figure 127.   Personal Strategy

Glossary

Those in charge of any organization — no matter how large or small — and those who aspire to hold leadership roles, are wise to use terms and phrases in precise ways in order to be clear about what they think, say, and do. This glossary compiles a number of such terms in one place for easy reference.

Term	Definition
Core Leadership Team (http://www.intelliven.com/note-on-core-leadership-teams/)	No one leader, and not even any two, has the breadth of competence and depth of capacity to do anything of much significance alone. Successful organizations often have a Core Leadership Team of **three to seven** top executives who are aligned to accomplish specific goals as a cohesive unit. The executives in a successful organization's Core Leadership Team are very **good at different important things;** they **enjoy working together**; all **want to accomplish the same thing and give credit for any success to others.**
How initiative is performing (http://www.intelliven.com/note-on-reviews-to-connect-the-top-of-the-house-to-the-front-line/)	Leaders should check on how well something important is going by regularly convening a forum of internal and external stakeholders for the one in charge of the activity to present: • What they are trying to do • What they have done towards that end • What has resulted from what they have done • What they have learned • What they plan to do next The reviewers ask clarifying questions and then offer their best advice to push up performance, provide guidance and perspective, and to be sure the best efforts from across the organization are brought to bear so as to increase the odds of the best possible result the soonest.
Leader	A leader **sets direction**, **aligns resources**, and **motivates action**. Another way to say it is that a leader **develops, holds, nurtures, communicates,** and **drives to achieve** a **vision**. Towards that end a leader: • Monitors and communicates a consolidated view of progress towards achieving the vision • Manages the resources of the organization for optimum long term growth and performance • Communicates what is to be done by whom • Provides resources and incentives needed to be successful
OD Perspective	OD can be viewed and applied from any of three principle perspectives: • that of the **leader** • the **inside consultant** to the leader • the **outside consultant** to the leader
Organization (http://en.wikipedia.org/wiki/Organization)	An organization is a social group which distributes tasks into systems that work together to achieve a collective goal or purpose. The word is derived from the Greek word organon, which is derived from the word ergon (as we know `organ) which means a compartment for a particular job.
Organization Development (http://www.american.edu/spa/msod/index.cfm)	Organization Development (or OD) is the systematic application of applied behavioral psychology tools, principles, and methods to intentionally evolve an organization from its current state to a specific next target state.

Term	Definition
Organization performance	We know how well an organization is doing by selecting performance measures and setting performance goals for those measures based on industry benchmarks for similar organizations at a similar stage of evolution, and doing similar things; performing; and then measuring results that are compared with: • **Targets** • **Past performance** • **Performance of other organizations** that are similar

Performance Improvement of Systems	Leaders systematically improve performance by
	
	• Projecting what will happen next
	• Executing
	• Measuring results
	• Comparing actual results to projections, and determining:
	  - Why actual results varied from projected results
	  - What is learned from the difference
	  - Making adjustments to the way things work and/or the way projections are made before repeating the entire process
	
	The comparison of actual to projected results is known as: **What-Why-So What-Now What**.

Purpose of an organization (http://www.intelliven.com/how-to-get-clear-about-what-problem-an-organization-solves-for-whom-how/)	The purpose of an organization is to solve a problem for a customer
Strategic Initiative	A Strategic initiative is what leaders have decided what is most important to be done next to change what is going on in order to increase the odds of winning.
Strategic Initiative components	For any strategic initiative it is important to know: • Where things are now (**current state**) • Why things need to change (**case for change**) • Where things will be once the intended change is completed (**target state**) • What must be done to get from the current state to the target state (the **strategic initiative**) • What will be hard about going from the current state to the target state (**barriers**)
Strategic Management	Strategic management is what is done to deliberately operate and develop the organization in a manner that is entirely consistent with its strategy.
Strategic Planning	Strategic planning is the structured process management uses to periodically engage leaders in reviewing and advancing their vision, assessing performance relative to goals, and advancing their strategy, including coming up with Strategic Initiatives for the coming performance period.
Strategic Thinking	Strategic thinking is how decisions and actions are made in the immediate-term in a manner mindful of long-term implications; that is, so as to be consistent with a strategy.
Strategy	Strategy is what people plan to do in order to win whatever game they are playing.
System	A system is a collection of resources working together to achieve a common goal.

Term	Definition
Systems of an organization (http://www.intelliven.com/what-an-organization-must-do-in-order-to-perform-and-grow/)	Every successful, growing organization has three core systems: Delivery system (**Do**) Demand Creation system (**Sell**) Capacity Development system (**Grow**)
Team	A small number of people (2 to 25) with complementary skills who are committed to a common purpose, goals, and approach for which they hold themselves mutually accountable. **Katzenbach & Smith, 1993: The Wisdom of Teams**
Why initiatives fail (http://www.galorath.com/wp/information-systems-risk-management-consortium-capers-jones-gary-gack-leon-kappelman-dan-galorath.php)	The number one reason initiatives fail is due to lack of management attention.

Exam questions

1. What is strategy?

   Strategy is what people plan to do in order to win whatever game they are playing.

2. What is strategic thinking?

   Strategic thinking is how decisions and actions are made in the immediate-term in a manner that is mindful of long-term implications; that is, so as to be consistent with a strategy.

3. What is strategic planning?

   Strategic planning is the structured process management uses to periodically engage leaders in advancing their strategy, including coming up with Strategic Initiatives.

4. What is a Strategic initiative?

   A strategic initiative is what must be done next to change what is going on in order to increase the odds of winning.

5. What is strategic management?

   Strategic management is what is done to deliberately operate and develop the organization in a manner that is entirely consistent with its strategy.

6. What is an organization?

   An organization is a social group which distributes tasks into systems that work together to achieve a collective goal or purpose. [The word is derived from the Greek word organon, which is derived from the word ergon (as we know òrgan) which means a compartment for a particular job.]

7. What is the purpose of an organization?

   The purpose of an organization is to solve a problem for a customer.

8. Give an example of an organization and explain what problem it solves for whom?

   See examples throughout the workbook, especially in the Get Clear section. Submit your answer using the template in Figure 11 (http://www.intelliven.com/templates/1596-2/) for feedback from the author or the author's students if desired.

9. What is a system?

   A system is a collection of resources working together to achieve a common goal.

10. What are the principle systems of an organization?

    Every successful, growing organization has three core systems: Delivery system (Do), Demand Creation system (Sell), and Capacity Development system (Grow).

11. How do you know how well an organization is performing?

    We know how well an organization is doing by selecting performance measures and setting performance goals for those measures based on industry benchmarks for similar organizations at a similar stage of evolution, and doing similar things; performing; and then measuring results that are compared with targets, past performance, and the performance of other organizations that are similar.

12. What is the role a leader?

A leader sets direction, aligns resources, and motivates action. Another way to say it is that a leader develops, holds, nurtures, communicates, and drives to achieve a vision. Towards that end a leader:

- Monitors and communicates consolidated view of progress towards achieving the vision
- Manages the resources of the organization for optimum long term growth and performance
- Communicates what is to be done by whom; provide resources and incentives they need to be successful

13. What are the key characteristics that define a core leadership team?

All the leaders in a successful organization's core team are very good at different important things; they enjoy working together; they all want to accomplish the same thing and give credit for any success to everyone else.

14. What is the number one reason initiatives fail?

The number one resaon initiatives fail is due to lack of management attention. Whatever would otherwise have gone wrong could most likely have been detected and tended to if management had paid attention along the way.

15. How do leaders systematically go about improving performance organization performance?

Leaders systematically improve performance by projecting how the organization will perform on its key measures, then they perform, then they measure actual performance and compare actual results to projected results and then determine why actual results varied from projected results, determine what is learned from the difference, and then make adjustments to the way things work and/or the way projections are made before repeating the entire process. This is called: What-Why-So What-Now What.

16. How should a leader check on how well something important (such as a strategic initiative) is going?

Leaders should check on how well something important is going by regularly convening a forum of internal and external stakeholders where the important activity's leader presents:

- what they are trying to do
- what they have done so far towards that end
- what has resulted from what they have done
- what they have learned so far
- what they plan to do next

The reviewers ask clarifying questions and then offer their best advice to push up performance, provide guidance and perspective, and to be sure the best efforts from across the organization are brought to bear so as to increase the odds of the best possible result the soonest.

17. What are the three different perspectives you can adopt when applying the lessons learned in Manage-to-Lead?

    Leader, inside consultant, outside consultant.

18. Which perspective will you use when applying what you have learned?

    Select conciously, purposefully, and wisely in every situation in order to drive to achieve the best possible results.

Made in the USA
San Bernardino, CA
20 December 2018